Phillip J. Donnelly

Rhetorical Faith:
The Literary Hermeneutics of
Stanley Fish

English Literary Studies
University of Victoria
2000

ENGLISH LITERARY STUDIES
Published at the University of Victoria

Founding Editor
Samuel L. Macey

ISBN 0-920604-75-7

The ELS Monograph Series is published in consultation with members of the Department by ENGLISH LITERARY STUDIES, Department of English, Univeristy of Victoria, P.O. Box 3070, Victoria, B.C., Canada v8w 3w1.

ELS Monograph Series No. 84
©2000 by Phillip Johnathan Donnelly

The cover shows a detail from Albrecht Dürer's *St. Jerome in his Study.*

Printed on acid-free paper, stitched, and bound by
MORRISS PRINTING COMPANY LTD.
Victoria, British Columbia

CONTENTS

Acknowledgments

Financial support from the Social Sciences and Humanities Research Council of Canada enabled me to take the time required to complete the research and writing involved in this project.

I am very grateful to Stanley Fish, for his persistence in raising important questions and for his consistently engaging work, written in a style that is always lucid. Even (and especially) where I disagree with him, I continue to benefit from what I have learned from his way of reading.

In writing this study I have become much indebted to the community of scholars in the English Department at the University of Ottawa. I am particularly grateful to the three people who read the manuscript in its entirety at different stages: David Jeffrey, Nicholas von Maltzahn and David Rampton. I thank David Jeffrey especially for his generous provision of wise and learned advice, as well as encouragement. I am grateful to Nicholas von Maltzahn for sharing the benefits of his erudition regarding all things Miltonic, as well as for his meticulous reading of the manuscript. To David Rampton I am thankful for responding to the manuscript in such a way that allowed him to share with me his passion for the craft of writing.

The late John Spencer Hill, friend, scholar, teacher, and Miltonist, read the first five chapters. I hope that he would have enjoyed reading the remaining chapters, and I offer them in honour of his memory. I am also grateful to Ashton Howley and Margo Simpson for reading and thoughtfully responding to specific parts of the manuscript.

Because it is not very common that this kind of work is willingly read by people who live and think primarily outside the academy, I am particularly thankful to Mark Czerwinski and Bruce and Heather Larratt for taking the time to read several chapters and send me their responses.

I thank Lorraine Weir at the University of British Columbia for introducing me to the work of Stanley Fish, and for providing me with encouragement at a turning point in my intellectual development. I am also very grateful to Michael Treschow at Okanagan University College, whose study of medieval literature continues to provide me with an outstanding example of scholarly integrity.

For their many years of support and encouragement, I am deeply grateful to my parents, Gordon and Patricia Donnelly. Above all, I thank my wife Nicole, who is stronger and more patient than she knows, for the depth of her care that is rooted in the same grace which enabled me to complete this project at all.

Abbreviations

Works by Stanley Fish:

SS	*Surprised by Sin*
SCA	*Self-Consuming Artifacts*
ITTC	*Is There a Text in this Class?*
DWCN	*Doing What Comes Naturally*
NSFS	*There's No Such Thing as Free Speech*
PC	*Professional Correctness*

Because I refer to two different works that have the same Latin title, *De Doctrina Christiana,* I have adopted the following system of abbreviations to distinguish between them, as well as between their respective translations:

DDC SAA	*De Doctrina Christiana.* Sanctus Aurelius Augustinus
OCD	*On Christian Doctrine.* Saint Augustine (Robertson trans.)
DDC IM	*De Doctrina Christiana.* Ioannes Miltonus.
CD	*Christian Doctrine.* John Milton (Carey trans.)

My use of these abbreviations should not, however, be taken to indicate my position with respect to the recent debate over whether Milton actually authored the theological treatise titled *De Doctrina Christiana.*

Introduction

Amid the many doubts that shape contemporary debates about literature, there persists the certainty that every reader employs an "interpretive strategy" of some kind. In shaping the consensus on this point,
the work of Stanley Fish has been particularly effective. Although he
most often writes from within the discursive imperatives of Milton studies or Renaissance literary scholarship, his arguments have become
influential across a wide range of disciplines as he has transposed his
analyses into broader theoretical claims. For example, in his recent
monograph, *Professional Correctness,* his arguments still include detailed
and specialized treatments of questions pertaining to Milton studies,
but the issues that he ultimately raises are important to anyone concerned with the effects of professionalism on the humanities. The
breadth of Fish's influence has resulted not only from his success in
persuading others concerning his specific claims, but also from his
capacity to broaden the appeal of those claims by drawing out the implications of his argument across disciplinary lines—even as he mounts an
argument against, for example, what is commonly understood as "inter-
disciplinarity." At a more basic level, his arguments are important
because he attempts to take the implications of accepting the primacy
of interpretive assumptions to their furthest extent. His writing, when
considered as a whole, represents a sustained attempt over several
decades to think through the most basic hermeneutic questions from
within the imperatives of discipline-specific arguments, rather than
lapsing into vague generalities. There have been singular critical
responses to Fish's various writings; however, despite the fact that he has
become one of the most influential literary critics in North America,
there has yet been no attempt to consider and engage his central theoretical arguments from within the terms of his own developing position.
The present study undertakes to offer precisely that kind of broader
consideration of his work.

The analysis here focuses on how Fish presents an *apologia* for his
theory of reader-response by linking his account of interpretive assumptions with the dynamics of "faith," or religious belief. He draws his
account of "faith" from a conflation of Augustinian and Miltonic theological discourse, although he ultimately rejects (as a matter of course)

11

both of their explicit interpretive positions. The great strength of Fish's own position derives from his structuring each argument in such a way that any attempt to challenge his specific literary or historical claims only serves to support his more general conclusion that such issues are always debatable. As a result, his arguments consistently end up making claims that are somehow independent of their specific literary or historical content. Because he maintains that our interpretive assumptions constitute the "text," there is no point in employing textual citations in an attempt to challenge his argument. Such citations would only provide further evidence that different interpretive assumptions are at work. As a result, the analysis of his arguments here will begin, not by challenging his "reading" of a given "text," but rather by drawing out the implications of accepting his position. In doing so, this study will address only those potential objections which emerge from within the terms of his own argument.

Because of the countless number of formal and informal interpretive strategies (or anti-strategies) available to readers, the continual challenge is how, or whether it is possible, to decide which strategy to employ in a given situation. In keeping with our condition as late moderns, the appearance of all these options is accompanied by the seeming inability to make judgments about their comparative value. Are some strategies better than others? Or are they only better for certain tasks in certain situations? If some strategies are more effective than others at achieving certain ends, can we decide what constitutes a worthy "end" for a given interpretation? The attempt to answer these questions cannot appeal to "texts" because part of the question hinges upon the issue of what constitutes a text in the first place. Similarly, the appeal to "different interpretations in different contexts" is no help, because the unique status of each context would make the idea of reading itself no different from self-projection or day-dreaming (whether the dreams belong to a group or an individual). Even if we were to conclude that "reading" is only self-projection, we would still be left to explain why we ever imagined there were two different activities instead of one. Yet why, among these multiple and multivalent uncertainties, does the very fact of the operation of interpretive assumptions somehow remain beyond doubt? Although we may not be able to avoid assuming something about the primacy of assumptions, we can conclude that there is at least no point in mounting an argument against the primacy of interpretive assumptions.

Nevertheless, we are still faced with the question of whether we can choose such assumptions. There is a sense in which everyone obviously does so, but Fish insists that such consciously "chosen" assumptions must always depend ultimately upon other assumptions which (although they too are constantly changing) are at least momentarily inaccessible (*ITTC* 367-71; *DWCN* 464). Fortunately, we are not concerned here with "unconscious assumptions," nor can we be, since the moment that they become objects of conscious thought they are no longer *un*conscious. Likewise, of the innumerable possible interpretive strategies among which a reader can choose on any given reading occasion, none is necessarily unconscious (although some claim the unconscious mind as an object of inquiry, such positions are themselves still usually held consciously). Can reader-response theory help us to discern better which of these strategies we should employ? At the same time, the inaccessibility of unconscious assumptions raises questions about the basic character of human freedom. Fish's generally anti-modern position clearly disavows all forms of rationalism upon which any genuine determinism could depend, but how does his account of inexorable yet inaccessible beliefs allow for the paradoxes of interpretive freedom or responsibility?

The attempt to understand how Fish extricates his position from any dependence upon the actual content of his own interpretation of Augustine or Milton results in a quasi-narrative argument in which the intelligibility of each step presupposes all that has come before it. Our examination of Fish's work begins, *in medias res,* at that point in *Is There a Text in this Class?* where he cites Augustine's rule of charity as evidence to support his own argument for the primacy of interpretive assumptions. Fish's interpretation of Augustine in that context leads us to consider his earlier and more extended treatment of Augustine's *De Doctrina Christiana,* offered in *Self-Consuming Artifacts.* From this assessment we discover not only how Fish handles Augustine in the development of his own position, but also how *Is There a Text?* continues and transforms the theoretical project begun in *Self-Consuming Artifacts.* Chapter 2 describes and assesses how Fish's notion of "faith," developed in the two earlier works, is clarified and defended in *Doing What Comes Naturally* and *There's No Such Thing as Free Speech.*

The next three chapters gradually retrace each step in Fish's central argument for the primacy of interpretive assumptions. Chapter 3 responds to Fish's reading of *De Doctrina Christiana,* attending specifically to his argument that Augustine's rule of charity cannot function as an interpretive constraint. How is Fish able to maintain such a position while simultaneously employing a stable (constrained) interpretation of that rule to support his own argument? Chapter 4 returns to his treatment of the topic of "rhetoric," in order to follow how he links the argument for the primacy of interpretive assumptions with the impossibility of judging between competing strategies. How does Fish re-orient the Augustinian idea of *fides quaerens intellectum* (faith seeking understanding) so that the actual content of the *fides* becomes constitutionally nonspecifiable? Chapter 5 then continues the comparative close reading of Augustine's *De Doctrina,* but with the preceding discussion of rhetoric (as well as Milton's *De Doctrina*) now in view, in order to draw out the full implications of Fish's attempt to render all accounts of faith "rhetorical."

With that detailed analysis of Fish's central arguments in place, the final two chapters bring a reconfigured account of charity and faith into direct engagement with the central points of continuity that remain evident in his more recent publications. In the sixth chapter we consider his account of professional literary practice in *Professional Correctness.* Given Fish's arguments for the inefficacy of charity as an interpretive constraint and for the rhetorical character of faith, it is appropriate to ask how his account of professional literary interpretation allows for alterity. Across the humanities, but especially among literature scholars, there is a deepening concern regarding the way in which the sheer demands of professional performance foster a blindness to alterity—not in the form of aggression, but in a *de facto* busy disregard of others which results in a general and persistent failure even to consider their needs. What does Fish's account of professionalism imply regarding the treatment of others?

Regarding my general approach to Fish's work, I offer two preliminary considerations. First, although I engage Fish's interpretation of specific passages from Augustine and Milton by drawing upon my own reading, the analysis nevertheless continues at each stage to draw out only the implications of accepting Fish's broader argument. The alternative readings that I offer do not depend upon a rejection of his main argument regarding the primacy of interpretive assumptions, nor do they depend upon rejecting the assumptions used in his own reading. Of course, it could be argued that, if my conclusions were to end up questioning Fish's interpretation, my reading must have made tacit use of different assumptions. Either that is the case, or my argument here already assumes that something other than interpretive assumptions can determine the resulting interpretation (thereby presupposing the answer to the question at issue). It might then seem that our acceptance of the belief in the primacy of interpretive assumptions will depend upon our assumptions—that is, people assume either that interpretive constraints go, as it were, "all the way down," or that they do not. But this alternative also depends upon the proposition it claims to hold in question, because it already construes the debate in terms of "assumptions." This kind of second-order question-begging conundrum on both sides is part of the reason why so many attempts to debate the issue of interpretive assumptions end up convincing no one of the opposing view. And yet, the persistent intelligibility of just such an account of the matter to *both* sides of the debate (regarding the primacy of interpretive assumptions) demonstrates that the disagreement is not simply a function of incommensurability. This investigation therefore attempts to broach the pivotal question of interpretive assumptions from an angle that makes the best use of that discursive sphere of mutual intelligibility (however small). Regardless then of how presumptuous it may seem, one of the ultimate aspirations of this investigation is to offer an account of the interpretive process that is intelligible to both sides of the debate and which yet avoids the conundrums inherent to both discourses in their totality.

Second, the historical considerations that I introduce in the third through fifth chapters develop out of the attempt to rethink each pivotal stage of Fish's argument. He introduces certain issues pertaining to medieval and Renaissance theology specifically because he finds them to be helpful analogues for his theoretical arguments. For example, he suggests that "even though 'theological' is a term of accusation in structuralist and poststructuralist rhetoric," the insights of both positions "have been anticipated by theological modes of reasoning" (*ITTC* 181). The middle chapters of this study are therefore concerned with the precise means by which Fish attempts to discern these modes of reasoning in the theological work of Augustine and Milton. This attempt to "slow down" the logical steps involved in Fish's argument is also part of the larger effort to understand exactly how he manages to remove his theoretical conclusions from any dependence upon the specific content of his own interpretation of Augustine. The general explanation would be the "second-order question-begging" described above, but how does Fish actually accomplish such distancing in this specific case? Among the "countless number" of interpretive approaches mentioned earlier, we could include the "Augustinian" mode. For this reason, our focus on Fish's reading of Augustine will also allow us to test whether reader-response theory can offer any clue regarding the possibility of judging between various reading strategies.

15

CHAPTER ONE

Dialectic

Is it possible to present a theory concerning the emergence of interpretive principles without depending upon assumptions which would
predetermine our assessment of such a theory? The primary difficulty
with such a question is that its coherence depends upon the belief that
our thinking can somehow be "stopped," in order to allow an objective
view of the interpretive process. The present interpretation of Fish's
reader-response theory will, therefore, attempt to focus specifically on
the developmental character, not only within Fish's position, but also
within our own interpretive engagement of his changing perspective.
Our first objective is to examine the deployment of Augustinian
hermeneutics within Fish's theory of reader response (as it first appears
in *Is There a Text in This Class?*), before examining his earlier reading of
Augustine in *Self-Consuming Artifacts*. The investigation will then focus
on his more recent work, in *Doing What Comes Naturally* and *There's No
Such Thing as Free Speech,* in order to see whether the same process dis-
covered in the earlier works continues to operate.

In *Is There a Text in This Class?* Fish employs Augustinian hermeneutics for both the articulation and defence of reader-response theory. In
the course of presenting the initial arguments to support his position,
Fish offers Augustine's interpretive theory as an example of a reading
strategy which leads to the "endless reproduction of the same text":

> Augustine urges just such a strategy, for example, in *On Christian Doctrine* where
> he delivers the "rule of faith" which is of course a rule of interpretation. It is daz-
> zlingly simple: everything in the Scriptures, and indeed in the world when it is
> properly read, points to (bears the meaning of) God's love for us and our
> answering responsibility to love our fellow creatures for His sake. If only you
> should come upon something which does not at first seem to bear this mean-
> ing, that "does not literally pertain to virtuous behaviour or to the truth of faith,"
> you are then to take it "to be figurative" and proceed to scrutinise it "until an
> interpretation contributing to the reign of charity is produced." (*ITTC* 170)

At this point in Fish's argument, the citation of Augustine's "rule of

16

faith" provides a classic example of a totalizing interpretive strategy. Fish goes on to cite similar systems which allow "the endless reproduction of the same text," such as psychoanalysis, Robertsonianism, numerology and "ordinary language" (170). From the existence of such totalizing strategies, the fact that such reading is possible, Fish argues that the perception of different formal texts only reflects the deployment of different interpretive strategies (169-70). Because our idea of what constitutes a given formal text results from our interpretive assumptions, the existence of any "text" at all must be equally dependent upon such assumptions (167). This does not imply, however, that there is no guard against "interpretive anarchy" (172). The fact that each reader belongs to an interpretive community whose members actually constitute ("write") the text by virtue of their shared interpretive assumptions, explains why there is often much consistency between some individual readings, as well as wide variation between groups (171).

This appeal to the existence of interpretive communities in order to defend his theory is the second way in which Fish employs Augustinian hermeneutics. The shift in usage is subtle yet critically important for his argument. In one sense, Fish seems to be simply extending his reading of *On Christian Doctrine* ("rule of faith" terms) onto his description of interpretive communities:

> If it is an article of faith in a particular community that there are a variety of texts, its members will boast a repertoire of strategies for making them. And if a community believes in the existence of one text, then the single strategy which the members employ will be forever writing it. . . . The assumption in each community will be that the other is not correctly perceiving the "true text," but *the truth* will be that each perceives the text (or texts) its interpretive strategies demand and call into being. (*ITTC* 171; emphasis added)

The shift in terminology, from "interpretive" communities to "faith" communities, is important within this passage, because it reflects the basis for Fish's own "truth" claim. Given his earlier assertion that there is no such thing as "pure perception" or an unmediated "fact" (166-68), how could he know the objective "truth" about interpretive strategies?

> The only stability, then, inheres in the fact (at least in my model) that interpretive strategies are always being deployed, and this means that communication is a much more chancy affair than we are accustomed to think. (172)

How could he purely observe the "fact" that interpretive strategies are always being used? By the terms of his own position, such unmediated observation (warranting universal status) is not possible. In order to

17

avoid a direct contradiction, Fish must base his factual claim on something other than observation, and this is precisely what he does:

> I am assuming, it is the article of my faith, that a reader will always execute some set of interpretive strategies and therefore perform some succession of interpretive acts. (169)

By basing his factual claim on "faith" rather than observation, he avoids a potential problem in logic; however, in doing so, he also makes his own theory simply one "faith system" among many. Because the success of the theory depends upon its power to explain all other faith communities (interpretive systems), such an inference will not be conceded, at least not at this stage in his argument. Although the term "faith" is not explicitly defined, his use of the word indicates those beliefs which are not simply "irrational," but are beyond the scope of rational demonstration because they are concerned with the very nature of what constitutes demonstration. His use of "faith" also allows him to avoid the problems associated with rationalist appeals to "self-evident first principles" or mathematical appeals to unprovable but necessary axioms. At this point in Fish's argument, however, the discourse of "faith" has expanded, from one example of a totalizing system, to include his own theory.

In order to guard his theory against subverting itself as another "faith" system, Fish presents a preemptive *apologia* for his credo through a series of solutions to textual/interpretive difficulties, which are finally only resolved by appealing to his idea of "interpretive strategies" (149-67). The problem is that he must later reject his own apologetics because of the theory itself:

> The moral is clear: the choice is never between objectivity and interpretation but between an interpretation that is unacknowledged as such and an interpretation that is at least aware of itself. It is this awareness that I am claiming for myself, although in doing so I must give up the claims implicitly made in the first part of this essay. There I argue that a bad (because spatial) model had suppressed what was really happening, but by my own declared principles the notion "really happening" is just one more interpretation. (*ITTC* 167)

From this position Fish assumes that he can "give up" the implicit claims in the earlier part of his argument while still accepting (and asking his readers to accept) the conclusions which he derives from those claims. More important, this "concession" in his argument conceals the way in which the rest of his evidence (concerning the "facts" of inter-

18

pretation) is just as dependent as the earlier part of his argument upon a claim to know what is "really happening." Because interpretive strategies are inescapable, and disinterested perception is not possible, the credo of reader-response faith replaces the old dichotomy of "objectivity vs. interpretation" with the new dichotomy of "unacknowledged interpretation vs. self-aware interpretation." The primary difficulty in Fish's use of this dichotomy is that he continually implies that it is *better* to be a self-aware interpreter, rather than an unreflective (deluded) interpreter. For if readers cannot access objective principles which would allow them to judge between competing interpretive strategies, then there is no justification for choosing self-aware interpretation over unacknowledged interpretation. If all assertions of objective perception are illusory, then the valorization of self-awareness is simply another form of interpretive self-deception.

This objection to reader-response theory is similar to one that Fish addresses directly in *Is There a Text?* The objection is that Fish's position engages in a "double game," which uses one theory when interpreting other texts, but then "tacitly" depends upon "communal norms" (universal claims) when discussing those very interpretations (*ITTC* 303). Fish responds by clarifying his position, and insisting that his theory does not imply that understanding is impossible (303), even going so far as to argue that pure unintelligibility "is an impossibility" (307). He bases his counter-argument on the existence of interpretive communities, by noting that all communication can occur only within a specific discursive context (interpretive community), and that any attempt to gain an understanding "that operates above or across situations" is simply illusory (304). The most revealing part of Fish's argument is his repeated suggestions about what those raising such objections "do not realize" (304). The use of the term "realize" reminds us that reader-response theory, in spite of itself, continually depends upon the universal claim that interpretive communities and practices exist:

> The ability to interpret is not acquired; it is constitutive of being human. What is acquired are the ways of interpreting and those same ways of interpreting can also be forgotten or supplanted, or complicated or dropped from favour. (172)

Although there is no single universal interpretive strategy, the theory cannot escape making the universal (factual) assertion that interpretive strategies of some kind are always being used. Even if we grant this claim as an "article of faith," it still implies that reader-response theory depends upon an objective truth which is beyond all interpretive communities, a meta-hermeneutic/theological claim—in effect, "The fact is there are no facts." Therefore, it seems that reader-response theory implies a simultaneous rejection of its own most basic assumptions.

As far as it goes, such an objection is justified if we allow the assumptions of what Fish calls the "spatial" modelling of formal logic (*ITTC* 167). The main problem with such an indictment is that it ignores Fish's repeated attempt to present an alternative to such spatial logic, by focusing on the temporal experience of understanding. If we admit these various premises and implications of reader-response theory, not as metaphysical axioms of mathematically precise transcendent truth, but as stages in a process which are part of a larger movement, we can see them as no longer contradictory but as part of a "dialectical" transformation (explained more fully below). In his preface to "Interpreting the *Variorum*," which appears half-way through *Is There a Text?* Fish indicates that precisely such a process is at work:

> The essay thus concludes with a perspective that is not at all the perspective with which it began, and it is from that perspective that the essays subsequent to this one are written. (148)

The "essay" in question began by attempting to demonstrate the inability of formalist analysis to account for the temporal experience of interpretation. However, recognizing the problems inherent in simply replacing the "factual" claims concerning texts with another set of factual claims about a reader's experience, Fish finally proposes the idea of interpretive communities as a way of accounting for interpretive stability without positing the formal existence of interpretive strategies (147-48). The new "perspective" (mentioned in the above quotation) is the idea of interpretive communities itself. This single insight allows Fish to defend his position against all challenges, but only at the cost of abandoning those premises which supported his initial inquiry. The repeated response to all objections against the primacy of interpretive assumptions is his positing of "interpretive communities" or "faith communities." According to Fish, the authority of interpretive communities renders impossible—in practice—both individual relativism and solipsism, because no one's most basic beliefs, whether moral or factual, can ever be held in isolation (318-20). Whether or not we accept Fish's argument against relativism at this point, we can already see that the entire theory of reader-response stands or falls on the existence of interpretive (or "faith") communities; and yet that assertion itself can only be accepted *as* an "article of faith."

Thus far we have postponed inquiry into the fact that Fish's view of Augustine's theory is itself an interpretation of *On Christian Doctrine*. Given

Fish's argument, we are prompted to ask what interpretive assumptions he employs in his reading of Augustine. According to Fish's theory, all that he could ever read in Augustine's works must always be a function of the interpretive assumptions that Fish holds. At the same time, Fish's most basic beliefs can only be a mixture of those shared/not shared by the various communities of which he is a member. Therefore, reader-response theory, insofar as it depends upon his reading of Augustine, is a function of those intersecting and evolving interpretive assumptions. But is it possible to discover the interpretive premises that Fish employs in his reading of Augustine?

One of these, at least, is particularly clear. Fish's attempt to classify Augustinian hermeneutics as simply one totalizing system among many depends at that very moment upon the ability of his own theory to conceal its totalizing claims through the appropriation of the discourse of "faith." Because Augustine's theory is used as an example, which is then absorbed into Fish's account of interpretive communities, Fish's own theory depends upon his reading of Augustine, to the extent that it depends upon the idea of interpretive communities. If Augustine's theory does not function as the totalizing system that Fish claims it to be, his own theory must still account for it as such. However, in addition to his insistence that the unrelenting fact of interpretive strategies (and therefore interpretive communities) can be accepted solely as an "article of faith," his theory is only defensible insofar as it offers an alternative to the metaphors of spatial logic that would refute it. The designation "spatial," as Fish uses it (*ITTC* 167), indicates the general way in which formal logic tends to equate all cognitive processes with deduction, thereby treating the objects of thought as reified universals. In an attempt to make eternally and immutably true propositions the primary objects of cognition, such logic emphasizes the ocular metaphors of knowledge, and in doing so suppresses the way in which all human understanding occurs only within a temporal (diachronic) framework. In the study of literature such thinking results in an emphasis upon the text as an "object," to the point of denying any value in a reader's experience (*SCA* 400-07). Fish earlier rejected such logic, because of its failure to account adequately for human experience (in reading or thinking), and attempted to develop his own alternative to such spatial metaphors in his notion of "dialectic." Before writing *Is There a Text in This Class?* Fish had already presented a more extended treatment of both Augustine's *On Christian Doctrine* and his own idea of "dialectic" in *Self-Consuming Artifacts*.

Although *Self-Consuming Artifacts* is concerned primarily with seventeenth-century prose styles, it begins by using Plato's *Phaedrus* and Augustine's *On Christian Doctrine* as paradigmatic texts for the entire proj-

21

ect. The central argument concerns an historical claim regarding the existence of an opposition between "rhetorical" and "dialectical" forms of "literary presentation" (*SCA* 1). The goal of this project is to produce "an explanation that does not explain away" (397). "Rhetorical" writing or speaking, in this argument, gives only a flattering reflection of the readers'/hearers' own biases, which amounts to comforting encouragement of existing assumptions and logic (1), while "dialectical" writing is "humiliating" but transforming. Dialectic leads to a "conversion" which is "not only a changing but an exchanging of minds" (2), as though a person moves from one way of seeing the world to another (3). Before having a dialectical experience, a person's perception is "discursive, or rational," such that entities are seen as discrete and logically ordered (3). After an experience of the transforming power of dialectic, perception is "anti-discursive and anti-rational," as "lines of demarcation between places and things fade in the light of an all embracing unity" (3). A "dialectical presentation" is "self-consuming," in that it attempts to use discursive rational forms to lead the reader to transcend those very forms and thereby abandon them. It breaks from the traditional claims made by art to represent "Truth," and attempts instead to "[point] away from itself to something its forms cannot capture" (4). The goal of a dialectical presentation is, therefore, not the "making of better poems" but the "making of better persons" (4). In addition to this main historical argument, Fish indicates that he is also trying to present implicitly a secondary theoretical argument, that "the proper object of [literary] analysis is not the work but the reader" (4). He only presents this argument explicitly in the Appendix, "Literature in the Reader" (discussed more fully below). How exactly does he arrive at this understanding of "rhetoric" and "dialectic," and the accompanying notion of a "self-consuming artifact"?

Fish begins by pointing out how "dialectic" operates in Plato's *Phaedrus,* before going on to show how the same process operates in a Christian context. The *Phaedrus* presents a "series of discrete conversations or seminars," which require that "to enter into the spirit and assumptions of any one of these self-enclosed units is implicitly to reject the spirit and assumptions of the unit immediately preceding" (*SCA* 9). As a result, the *Phaedrus* begins by attempting to distinguish good writing from bad writing, but ends up rejecting the value of writing altogether (8, 15). Fish argues that such a conclusion accords with the movement of the entire dialogue, because this final rejection, "far from contradicting what has preceded, corresponds exactly to what the reader, in his repeated abandoning of successive stages in the argument, has been doing" (13). Rather than leading a listener or reader through a series of logically necessary steps, which may still lead to a false conclusion, the dialectical process attempts instead to raise the auditor "up to a vision, to a point where his understanding is so enlarged that he can see the truth immediately, without the aid of a mediating process or even of an orator" (12). There are two elements worth noting at this point: first, Fish's ability to discern a "dialectical" process at work in the dialogue is dependent upon his close attention to the experience of the reader (13); second, this reading is unusual insofar as it associates formal logic and discursive practices with rhetoric rather than philosophy. Normally readings of Platonic texts link rhetoric with the appeal to disorderly passions rather than to any objectivist epistemology. Conversely, Platonic dialectic is usually associated with the ultimate goal of rational order (in the soul and state), and usually emphasizes the rigorously logical/mathematical nature of the form of the Good. Fish is able to avoid this standard interpretation on the grounds that "rhetoric tends to canonize the status quo" (*SCA* 15). By linking objectivist epistemology with the complacency of the existing order (because of its claims to "common sense" etc.), Fish is able to oppose the dialectical method of the philosopher with the "rational" method of the rhetorician. The importance of this set of categories within the development of Fish's theory will be explored more fully later, but at this point we can see that it allows Fish to group Plato and Augustine together, thereby eliding any distinctions between them which may contradict his reading.

Fish begins his reading of Augustine's *On Christian Doctrine* by implicitly presenting himself as an apologist for Augustinian hermeneutics to modern readers: "To the modern literary sensibility, the least acceptable tenet in Augustine's teaching on the interpretation of the Bible is likely to be his theory of figurative reading" (*SCA* 21)—i.e., the "rule of faith," whose end is charity. Fish goes on to attempt an explanation of this "least acceptable tenet," but the rhetorical machinery (to opposite effect) has already been set in motion by this gesture. His attempt to make the "rule of faith" "acceptable" to modern sensibilities only serves to heighten the sense of strangeness surrounding Augustine's view. Fish presents the following quotations from Augustine's work:

> Whatever appears in the divine Word that does not literally pertain to virtuous behaviour or to the truth of faith you must take to be figurative. (*OCD* 3.10.14)

> Therefore in the consideration of figurative expressions a rule such as this will serve, that what is read should be subjected to diligent scrutiny until an interpretation contributing to the reign of charity is produced. (*OCD* 3.15.23)

Fish points out that "this rule would seem to urge us to disregard context, to bypass the conventional meanings of words, and, in general, to violate the integrity of language and discursive forms of thought" (*SCA*

22). Recognizing that, "from the point of view of our normal assumptions about the world and our perceptions of it," Augustine's theory may seem "wholly subversive" (21), Fish attempts to explain that, for Augustine, the inability to see the love of God in every passage of Scripture (and every part of the world) is a "problem of perception," an inability to "see" the truth as it really is (22). As with the process of dialectic in Plato's *Phaedrus*, Augustine's goal is to achieve a unifying vision. Categories of distinction are continually collapsed so that wherever the believer "may find truth, it is the Lord's" (*OCD* 2.18.28; *SCA* 28), because a "pure and healthy internal eye" will always produce "interpretations contributing to the reign of charity" (*SCA* 29). Fish argues that this same collapsing of distinctions is incarnated in the last book of Augustine's treatise, where he introduces the categories of classical rhetoric merely to subvert them and to show that they are redundant (*OCD* 4.1.2-4.5.8; *SCA* 30-34). Each step in the analysis of rhetorical practice is placed in a dialectical relation to the step which precedes it. Initially eloquence is rejected in favour of wisdom, then wisdom in speaking is reduced simply to knowing the words of Scripture (*SCA* 37), as each stage of the discussion further subsumes rhetoric within the truth it would present.

Finally, Fish argues that the last stage of *On Christian Doctrine* involves, like the *Phaedrus*, a rejection of all that has gone before, as Augustine points out that the speaker should simply "pray that God may place a good speech in his mouth" (4.30.63). Such extreme dependence upon God effectively makes not only the study of rhetoric but also the human speaker/writer superfluous (the height of dialectical self-negation) (*SCA* 38). This does not imply, however, that Augustine thinks preaching should stop (*OCD* 4.18.35; *SCA* 40). The activity must be carried out with the knowledge that, although the labour of a preacher does not derive importance from being "efficacious or necessary," it is still valuable as an opportunity to serve God (*SCA* 40). Because of the need to avoid the two extremes of pride and despair, the interpretation and presentation must be simultaneously "assertive and self-effacing" (40). Once again, Fish's ability to see a "dialectical process" at work depends primarily upon his focus on the reader's experience of *On Christian Doctrine*. Fish finds the few potentially explicit references to a dialectical process in Augustine's description of spiritual development (transformative aspect of dialectic) (*OCD* 2.7.9-11; *SCA* 23) and in his use of the "travel motif" to describe the journey of faith (*OCD* 1.4.4; *SCA* 24). We shall return later to look more closely at both of these passages from *On Christian Doctrine*, but at this point, rather than challenge Fish's reading of Augustine, we can already begin to see how his interpretation provides a dialectical starting point for his later work.

Fish ends his analysis of *On Christian Doctrine* by inferring from his interpretation what a sermon might look like if it were based upon these dialectical principles. The strategy of such a sermon would be to "open eyes" to a new vision of reality rather than gain assent to a particular set of propositions (*SCA* 41). The presentation would subvert conventional discursive syntax and its distinctions between grammatical elements, and in doing so, attempt to gesture towards that which its own grammatical constructs cannot contain (41). As a result, the structure of the whole sermon would be self-consuming in such a way that it could bring into question the frame of reference created by those assumptions which are shared (at least initially) by the listeners and the speaker (42). Finally, the sermon will "give itself over to God," living within the paradoxical balance between faith and presumption (42). Using these characteristics to define the "self-consuming artifact," Fish then proceeds to cite instances of such dialectical presentations among various works of seventeenth-century prose. He eventually concludes, however, that the opposition between "rhetorical" and "dialectical" is not simply a difference in prose styles, but "an opposition of epistemologies," such that rhetoric "leads the auditor or reader step-by-step, in a logical and orderly manner, to a point of certainty and clarity," while dialectic "undermines certainty and moves away from clarity, complicating what had at first seemed perfectly simple, raising more problems than it solves" (*SCA* 378). The reason for the self-consuming style being largely abandoned by the end of the seventeenth century is the widespread acceptance of the belief in rationally accessible objective truth (380). Self-consuming artifacts were predicated on the belief that divine truth is ultimately inaccessible to human reason (380). Because of the epistemological shift towards objectivist rationalism and the accompanying faith in human reason to discover all divine truth, only the "self-satisfying" or "plain" style of prose survived into the eighteenth century (380-81).

We can now return to the earlier question of whether it is possible for us to discern the interpretive assumptions at work in Fish's reading of Augustine, a reading that goes on to play such an important role in the development of reader-response theory. The Appendix to *Self-Consuming Artifacts*, entitled, "Literature in the Reader," states explicitly some of the interpretive assumptions that Fish uses. What characterizes his approach is the belief that "meaning" is a sequential process that "happens" to the reader rather than something which is contained in formal semantic or stylistic units (*SCA* 386-88):

What makes problematical sense as a statement makes perfect sense as a strategy, as an action made upon a reader rather than as a container from which a reader extracts a message. (384)

This view of reading changes the central textual/interpretive question from "What does it mean?" to "What does it do?" (390). Within such a view, there is no substitute for the reader's subjective temporal reading experience (393). Even a moment's reflection by the same reader upon the immediately previous experience results in stopping the "meaning" (395). We can see the importance of this interpretive approach for Fish's historical argument, in that he does not primarily attempt to show that Plato or Augustine explicitly endorses the practice which he calls "dialectic." Instead, each step of the argument depends upon an implicit consensus regarding the experience of "the reader" in attending to the work. In this way, the focus upon a reader's temporal experience informs his historical argument regarding the existence of "dialectical" versus "rhetorical" presentations. This relationship persists in spite of Fish's suggestion to the contrary:

> I do not ask my readers to commit themselves to this [implicit theoretical] position or even to consider it, if they find the issues it raises uninteresting or distracting. (*SCA* 4)

Fish is technically correct in suggesting that the historical thesis is not logically dependent as a formal argument upon the success of the appended theoretical argument. However, the real effectiveness of this statement is in the way that his disclaiming of the theoretical argument draws our attention away from the operation of that very theory in dictating the interpretive assumptions of the historical argument. Because the theoretical argument informs the reading which produces his historical argument, a rejection of his argument for "literature in the reader" would mean that the historical argument could also be abandoned. Thus the appearance of choice, as though his readers could decide whether or not they prefer to be blind to his appended interpretive assumptions, is completely misleading.

At this stage in the development of Fish's position, although the reader and text are inseparable and dynamically interdependent (*SCA* 411), they are treated as essentially stable categories. As Fish later notes (in *Is There a Text?*), our most basic interpretive assumptions are necessarily inaccessible to us at that moment when they are in operation (*ITTC* 360). Any attempt to objectify our most basic assumptions can only be predicated upon the simultaneous concealment of other premises (360). This is why the Appendix to *Self-Consuming Artifacts* does not provide the opportunity that it seems initially to offer, in leading us to think that Fish can really tell us about his interpretive assumptions. Only later, when he no longer holds those assumptions, can Fish objectify and identify them as previously inaccessible beliefs.

This shift in his most basic interpretive assumptions leads us to consider the ways in which *Is There a Text?* shares a dialectical relationship with the earlier work in *Self-Consuming Artifacts:*

> What interests me about many of the essays collected here is the fact that I could not write them today. I could not write them today because both the form of their arguments and the form of the problems those arguments address are a function of assumptions which I no longer hold. (*ITTC* 1)

If, by the time that he writes the Introduction, he no longer holds the assumptions upon which the work initially proceeded, what supports his conclusions? The problem with such a question is that it assumes the criteria of the same spatial logic that Fish argues is incomplete by its own terms of reference. The inability of such logic to account for subjective reading experience eventually led him to the conclusion that giving greater attention to the temporal or sequential dimension of reading provides a better account of the perceived objectivity of the text, rather than vice versa. As a result, the answer to such a question would be that, instead of employing a formal logical structure whose conclusions are all deduced from their premises, the main argument of *Is There a Text?* recounts how Stanley Fish came to discover the importance of interpretive communities—in effect, how he came to "faith." Earlier we noted how a central essay in *Is There a Text?* demonstrates a dialectical development within itself, but now we can begin to see how the entire collection is a self-consuming artifact. The assumptions in the early essays of *Is There a Text?*—which he eventually ends up rejecting— are the same unacknowledged premises upon which the argument of *Self-Consuming Artifacts* is predicated:

> Without that assumption—the assumption that the text and the reader can be distinguished from one another and that they will hold still—the merits for their rival claims could not have been debated and an argument for one or the other [reader vs. text] could not have been made. (*ITTC* 1)

Is There a Text? is, therefore, "dialectical" in its relationship to the argument of *Self-Consuming Artifacts,* but it is also a self-consuming artifact with respect to its own development. In this sense, *Is There a Text?* is an attempt to embody ("incarnate") the argument of *Self-Consuming Artifacts.*

The differences, however, between the interpretive assumptions of the two works extend far beyond the explicit questions concerning belief in a stable text and reader. In *Self-Consuming Artifacts* Fish argues that the rise of objectivist epistemology at the close of the seventeenth century meant the end of such dialectical presentations (*SCA* 380-81). The ability to write/read a self-consuming artifact was predicated upon a belief in the *in*ability of human reason to access divine truth. Notwithstanding the limitations of human reason (i.e., rejection of foundationalist epistemology), a dialectical presentation still presupposed the accessibility (albeit non-rational) and objective existence of some divine truth. Where does this leave Fish's own self-consuming argument? The very existence and intelligibility of *Is There a Text?* serves as evidence that a general movement away from objectivist epistemology had already begun, within Fish's interpretive community, at the time of his writing. However, if dialectical presentations are always trying to gesture toward that which they cannot contain, thereby leading us into a transformative experience of finally seeing the unifying truth, we need to ask what kind of new "vision" this presentation invokes. Toward what "unifying truth" does this self-consuming artifact gesture?

The easy answer to such a question is the book's subtitle: "The Authority of Interpretive Communities." However, according to the models that Fish provides, the truth of a self-consuming artifact is not (cannot be) stated explicitly and can only be discerned by focusing on the dynamic process of reading. So, what is it like to read *Is There a Text in This Class?* What kind of "conversion" does it inspire? The experience does, indeed, give rise to "a whole new perspective." It allows us to see everything (text and world) as a construction of competing interpretive strategies, which are themselves only functions of continuously evolving social constraints. The process of reaching this new perspective involves what might be called a "threefold dialectic." We can see this development most clearly if we look at the one essay which explicitly links the arguments of *Self-Consuming Artifacts* with that of *Is There a Text?* "Structuralist Homiletics" appears in *Is There a Text?* but it effectively represents Fish's attempt to include one of Lancelot Andrewes's sermons among the self-consuming artifacts of seventeenth-century prose (*ITTC* 181, 194-96). Initially this chapter reads like a repetition of his earlier argument in *Self-Consuming Artifacts*, until we recall that the broader development of *Is There a Text?* will lead to the abandonment of the premises upon which the earlier argument depended:

> In Andrewes's theology the self is constituted not by a system [or structural function] but by the indwelling presence of Jesus Christ; but the effect of

28

the two ways of thinking is the same, to deny the distinction between the knower and the object of knowledge that is so crucial to a positivist epistemology. (*ITTC* 181)

The collapsing of the distinction between knower and object directly parallels Fish's own removal of the distinction between reader and text. In this way, not only does this essay offer yet another historical example of a dialectical work, but it does so as part of a larger dialectical process which transcends the premises with which Fish's argument begins. This self-reflexivity is simultaneously operating at yet another level, because the specific assumptions regarding the stability of text and reader which he is in the process of "dialectically transcending" are the very ones upon which his initial definition of dialectic depended. It would be easy to argue that this is simply a series of self-contradictions, but such an objection would depend on the false assumption that Fish held all of these positions simultaneously. Fish's argument is temporal rather than spatial, in that the operation of one set of premises gives rise to an insight, a literally "im-mediate" perception of truth (accepted only as an article of faith), which allows us then to adopt the new perspective in a way that is logically independent of the previous premises.

The successful incarnation of a dialectical process, however, is only achieved at the cost of abandoning the claim to "know" what dialectic is. Thus Fish's use of dialectic results in not so much a "new vision" as a "new blindness." The blindness is restricted, however, to our most basic interpretive assumptions. The very existence of the Appendix to *Self-Consuming Artifacts* testifies to Fish's earlier belief that there was some value in being able to objectify his interpretive assumptions. However, by the end of *Is There A Text?* he insists that such objectification is not possible:

> Now one might think that someone whose mind had been changed many times would at some point begin to doubt the evidence of his sense, for, after all, "this too may pass," and "what I see today I may not see tomorrow." But doubting is not something one does outside the assumptions that enable one's consciousness; rather doubting, like any other mental activity, is something that one does within a set of assumptions that cannot at the same time be the object of doubt. That is to say, one does not doubt in a vacuum but from a perspective, and that perspective is itself immune to doubt until it has been replaced by another which will be similarly immune. (*ITTC* 360)

Although we cannot objectify the most basic assumptions that we hold at present, we can acknowledge that all our factual claims are interpretations, and the virtue of being able to make this acknowledgment is the one insight upon which the blindness is predicated (167). Given the inacces-

29

sibility of interpretive assumptions, how can people "know whether or not" they are members "of the same interpretive community"?

> The only "proof" of membership is fellowship, the nod of recognition from someone in the same community, someone who says to you what neither of us could ever prove to a third party: "we know." I say it to you now, knowing full well that you will agree with me (that is, understand) only if you already agree with me. (173)

Once again, Fish privileges the stance of faith in his use of the term "fellowship," but more importantly, this passage demonstrates how the inaccessibility of interpretive assumptions (as Fish defines them) erases the distinction between understanding and agreement. If understanding is only possible between people who share in common at least some of their most basic inaccessible interpretive assumptions, all disagreements with "outsiders" are irrevocably incommensurable. Conversely, if two people really do share some of the same assumptions, they must to that same degree not only understand one another but must also agree with one another. This allows Fish to answer those who argue that other people can help us to access the operations of our most basic assumptions, by pointing out that insofar as we understand one another, we must share the same inaccessible assumptions and must be equally blind to the assumptions of one another. Therefore, we cannot even begin to question those inaccessible assumptions upon which Fish's own theory is predicated, because the extent to which we understand his position is the same extent to which we must share those same inaccessible beliefs.

The equation between "agreement" and "understanding" further implies that the will (volition) plays no role in understanding, or rather, that there is no distinction between the activities. "Ignorance" (unshared assumptions) is the only possible basis for perceptions of moral transgression. The idea that "choice" could somehow play a role in knowledge is so far from consideration that Fish is able to use the absurdity of such thinking to mock the project of objectivist epistemology in general:

> To someone who believes in determinate meaning, disagreement can only be a theological error. The truth lies plainly in view, available to anyone who has eyes to see; but some readers *choose* not to see it and perversely substitute their own meanings for the meanings that texts obviously bear. Nowhere is there an explanation of this waywardness (original sin would seem to be the only relevant model), or of the origin of these idiosyncratic meanings (I have been arguing that there could be none), or of the reason why some readers seem to be exempt from the general infirmity. (*ITTC* 338; emphasis added)

Given that complete unintelligibility is not possible, varying degrees of unintelligibility must be the only source of disagreement. The extent of agreement/understanding must then be a function of the mixture of shared and unshared interpretive assumptions. As a result, while all claims to "objectivity" only conceal "biases" (caused by assumptions etc.), the idea of individual motivation is nevertheless inoperative because volition, or "free choice," does not exist. The process which began by rejecting formalism, because of its inability to account for subjective reading experience, ends up making the subjective experience of choice nothing more than a node on the matrix of socio-linguistic determinism (cf. Meynell 6-7). Of course, such a radically constrained view of subjectivity does not correspond with anyone's subjective experience, and Fish makes this same point as he concludes: "the position I have been presenting is not one which you or anyone else could live by" (*ITTC* 370).

What Fish occludes, however, is that the admitted inapplicability of his account results from the way his belief in inaccessible assumptions entails a tacit return to formalist logic. The only way to defend the claim that the operation of our interpretive assumptions is predicated upon their inaccessibility is to introduce another "article of faith" which would give universal status to that inaccessibility. Obviously, as Fish maintains, we can never access all of our assumptions simultaneously; but that does not preclude being able to view various sets of assumptions critically through one another in a temporal sequence. This is hardly a plausible solution, in that it requires a potentially infinite regress of self-reflexivity, but as an alternative it shows how Fish's position depends upon ascribing ontological status to an absence. In so far as these interpretive assumptions can never be known *as* the inaccessible realities that Fish says they are, his entire theory (faith) is a theology of the unknown god(s). The existence of interpretive assumptions may, therefore, be granted as an article of faith, but the object of this "faith" is a reality which is constituted by absence. If the ascription of divine status to these inaccessible premises seems too far-fetched, we need only to compare an earlier quoted passage from *Is There a Text?* with a passage from *Surprised by Sin:*

> Milton's point here is one he will make again and again; all acts are performed in God's service; what is left is the choice between service freely rendered and service exacted against his will. (*SS* 18)

> The moral is clear: the choice is never between objectivity and interpretation but between an interpretation that is unacknowledged as such and an interpretation that is at least aware of itself. (*ITTC* 167)

31

The Miltonic sovereignty of God has been replaced by the inaccessible and inescapable interpretive assumptions which shall be served, willingly or not. Are these assumptions the "divine truth" towards which Fish's own theory dialectically gestures?

Part of the resilience (or implacability) of Fish's theory results from his conflation of different senses of the term "faith." Although the notion of "faith" is first taken from his description of totalizing interpretive systems like Augustinian hermeneutics, when he applies the term to "inaccessible assumptions" he has necessarily shifted to a second definition, because the first referred only to objectifiable systems. His insistence upon the impossibility of deciding between competing interpretations (*ITTC* 340) depends upon eliding the distinction between these two uses of the term "faith," because if he consistently used the second definition the theory would bear no relation to any subject/object of human consciousness. Fish might respond to such an objection by arguing that, although such "faith" systems (in the first sense) may be objectifiable, the choice between systems will always be predicated upon assumptions which are at that moment inaccessible. This leads us to the third sense in which he uses the term "faith," because the very existence of such deeply rooted assumptions ("faith" premises) can only be accepted as an article of "faith." This three-fold sense of "faith" allows Fish to assert an unprovable belief (faith no. 3) in inaccessible and inescapable assumptions (faith no. 2) upon which our objectifiable interpretive principles (faith no. 1) depend. By shifting between these different uses of the term, Fish can defend his position by adopting whichever sense allows him to avoid creating a contradiction within the assumptions of a given objection. He can use the term to refer to objectifiable beliefs when discussing other positions, but all challenges to the belief in interpretive communities or strategies can be answered by simply invoking the god(s) of agnosis, thereby claiming immunity for his theory by virtue of its association with the inaccessible assumptions which allegedly constitute/deconstitute its object of inquiry.

In one sense, the argument of *Is there A Text?* is only a further development and defence of the idea of "literature in the reader" (and, by implication, the historical argument of *Self-Consuming Artifacts*), but it also ends up rejecting the notions of "reader" and "text" which the earlier work assumed. "Reader-response theory," as such, ends simultaneously with the close of *Is There a Text?* because there is no longer an object of "response" or an individual consciousness which can freely "respond." This results in more than simply "transcending" the premises of the earlier work, because both his idea of dialectic (self-consuming) and his reading of Augustine are based on those very interpretive assumptions which he later rejects. Where does that leave his reading of Augustine's *On Christian Doctrine*? Given the dependence of Fish's theory upon an appropriation of Augustine's view, what does the status of Fish's reading of *On Christian Doctrine* imply for reader-response theory? Chapter Three will attempt to answer these questions, by comparing my own reading of Augustine's *On Christian Doctrine* with that of Fish. The more immediate question is whether the notion of "interpretive communities" is itself simply another dialectical stage which is soon transcended, or whether the pantheon of agnosis continues to animate the dialectical process. The next chapter will therefore examine how Fish develops the implications that follow from such a faith in the unknowable.

CHAPTER TWO

Faith

Although there are some shifts in Fish's interpretive assumptions, between *Is There a Text?* and *Doing What Comes Naturally*, the changes hardly constitute a "dialectical transformation." In many respects, the later essays simply apply the implications of the "unifying vision" that Fish achieves in *Is There a Text?* and allow him to align himself more directly with those who oppose formalist and foundationalist epistemologies. Even the title, *Doing What Comes Naturally*, is simply an expansion of the idea of interpretive assumptions and communities, to include "the unreflective actions that follow from being embedded in a context of practice":

> This kind of action—and in my argument there is no other—is anything but natural in the sense of proceeding independently of historical and social formations; but once those formations are in place (and they always are), what you think to do will not be calculated in relation to a higher law or an overarching theory but will issue from you as naturally as breathing. In the words of John Milton, "from a sincere heart"—that is, a heart embedded in a structure of conviction—"unimpos'd expressions" will come "unbidden into the outward gesture." (*DWCN* ix)

The "context of practice" is in one sense only a more elaborate version of the "interpretive community," but the invocation of Milton is also consistent with Fish's earlier view, in that the eternal and omnipresent "context of practice" makes *in*sincerity an impossibility. Insincerity presupposes the notion of a free will that can choose whether or not to be honest. The new key term in *Doing What Comes Naturally* is "constraint," which is used interchangeably with "belief, or community, or practice" (33). Although the book does not make the same use of the Augustinian "rule of faith," this equation of terms makes "constraint" identical with "faith." Indeed, one of the "higher perspectives" that develops out of *Doing What Comes Naturally* is Fish's recognition that the defence of his position still depends upon the multiple senses of the term "belief" (or "faith"):

Either I am facing those who wish to identify a rationality to which *beliefs* or community practices would be submitted for judgment, or I am facing those who find in the deconstruction of that rationality the possibility of throwing off those *beliefs* and practices that now define us. When I argue against the first group, *beliefs* are forever escaping the constraints that rationality would impose; when I argue against the second group, *beliefs* are themselves constraints that cannot be escaped. Neither stance [in response to either group] delivers a finely tuned picture of the operations of *belief* (or community or practice) because that is not my task, and indeed it is a task which, if taken seriously (as it certainly should be), would prevent me from doing what I have tried to do. Whether I have done it and whether it was worth doing are questions that are happily not mine either to ask or to answer. (*DWCN* 32-33; emphasis added)

The "it" which he has "done" refers to the twofold response that runs throughout his arguments in *Doing What Comes Naturally,* as he consistently argues that the rejection of formalism does not imply relativism, but that post-structuralist "theory hope" is equally unfounded. At the end of the previous chapter we observed three different senses of the term "faith" between which Fish continually shifts his argument. We can see in the above passage that he uses the first definition (objectifiable totalizing system) to address the foundationalists, by arguing that rationality itself is just one among several competing faith systems. He then uses the second definition of "faith" (inaccessible and inescapable assumptions) to address the anti-foundationalists, by arguing that they can never be "free" from constraints of some kind. In this way, Fish places himself in opposition to both sides of the formalist/anti-formalist debate (as normally conceived), by taking the anti-formalist position so consistently that it cannot provide a new "foundation" from which to think or act. Significantly, there is no mention of his third use of the term "faith" to underwrite the very acceptance of those claims upon which the other two senses of the term "faith" depend (q.v. 32 above). As Fish observes, he never develops "a finely tuned picture of the operations of belief," and indeed, the attempt to do so would have kept him from the work that he does do (33). Whether it be the constraints of time or rhetorical coherence (or both) that keep Fish from undertaking the task, the present inquiry attempts just such an examination of "the operations of belief," specifically as they bear upon the formulation of Fish's own position where a faith in those operations of belief plays such a central role.

It is not necessary to rehearse the ways in which Fish repeatedly makes this same two-sided argument in different contexts, ranging from linguistic formalism and legal studies to psychoanalysis, rhetoric, and political change. The argument in each case amounts to the same double attack, which first collapses the distinction between "truth" and "bias," by demonstrating that both are only competing "normative obligations," but then pointing out that because we cannot escape the operation of contextual constraints which claim universal status, "all preferences are principled" (*DWCN* 11). This provides Fish with an opportunity to clarify his earlier argument, in that his insistence that all claims are based on contextually determined assumptions is balanced by the equal insistence that the recognition of such "circumstantiality" cannot keep anyone (including himself) from holding beliefs as though they were "universally true" (467). In this respect, *Doing What Comes Naturally* is an attempt to answer those objections against *Is There a Text?* which pointed out the apparent contradiction in simultaneously making and disallowing universal claims.[1]

This leads to a more important shift between the two works, in that *Doing What Comes Naturally* abandons the earlier attempt to privilege critical self-awareness, admitting that such awareness is both "impossible and superfluous" (464):

> It is impossible because there is no action or motion of the self that exists apart from the "prevailing realm of purposes" and therefore no way of achieving distance from that realm; and it is superfluous because the prevailing realm of purposes is, in the very act of elaborating itself, turning itself into something other than it was. (464)

Earlier, we noted that the attempt to valorize "self-awareness" in *Is There a Text?* (167) could only be the height of self-deception, and Fish now makes this same point, describing any such attempt at self-awareness as "a persuasive agenda that dare not speak its name" (*DWCN* 464). However, the above passage also implicitly demonstrates the connection between privileging critical self-consciousness and the belief in a "free individual," and, in this respect, shows how his earlier rejection of such individualism necessitates the later rejection of self-awareness. All of these clarifications and developments within his position are still consistent with the central article of faith, that interpretive strategies are both inaccessible and inescapable. The primary difference seems to be only in regard to a deepening recognition of the extent to which these inaccessible "constraints" continually influence us. There remains, however, a striking resemblance between the "persuasive agenda that dare not speak its name," and the inaccessible premises upon which Fish's theory is predicated. Can the unknown gods speak their names?

The mention of "theory" reminds us that not only are the terms "reader" and "response" no longer applicable to Fish's position, but neither any longer is the term "theory" (the self-consumption continues). In realizing the full implications of thinking in terms of constraints, Fish argues that "theory," as a meta-hermeneutic project, is not possible. Beginning with a definition of theory (taken from Knapp and Michaels), as "the attempt to govern interpretations of particular events by appealing to an account of interpretation in general" (*DWCN* 315), he concludes that "anti-foundationalism really isn't a theory at all; it is an argument against the possibility of theory" (*DWCN* 322). In one sense this position is simply a reiteration and clarification of his earlier conclusion (in *Is There a Text?*) that his theory has no consequences. Even so, at that point it was at least a "theory" without consequences. This clarification allows Fish to make more explicit his attempt to argue that anti-foundationalism is not simply a contradiction which depends upon making claims of universal status that it denies to all others. Ultimately, both his argument that anti-foundationalist theory has no consequences and his argument that relativism is impossible share the same premises. Both are based on the realization that, just as there are no universal truths, we cannot live as though such a position were universally true.

This is why Fish can insist that the usual argument against cultural relativism is wrong because "it mistakes the nature of the anti-foundationalist claim" (29). The usual argument takes anti-foundationalism to be the insistence that "there are no truths of moral significance that hold across cultures" (29). From this, the opponents deduce that either the claim must be held as universally true (thereby contradicting itself), or else held as a "local belief" and therefore not universally true (29). However, such an argument, according to Fish, is based on false premises:

> First of all, it mistakes the nature of the anti-foundationalist claim, which is not that there are no foundations, but that whatever foundations there are (and there are always some) have been established by persuasion, that is, in the course of argument and counter-argument on the basis of examples and evidence that are themselves cultural and contextual. Anti-foundationalism, then, is a thesis about how foundations emerge, and in contradistinction to the assumptions that foundations do not emerge but simply *are*, anchoring the universe and thought from a point above history and culture, it says that foundations are local and temporal phenomena, and are always vulnerable to challenges from other localities and other times. This vulnerability also extends, of course, to the anti-foundationalist thesis itself, and that is why its assertion does not involve a contradiction, as it would if what was being asserted was the impossibility of foundational assertion; . . . anti-founda-

37

tionalism can without contradiction include itself under its own scope and await the objections one might make to it; and so long as those objections are successfully met and turned back by those who preach anti-foundationalism (a preaching and a turning back I am performing at this moment), anti-foundationalism can be asserted as absolutely true since (at least for the time being) there is no argument that holds the field against it. (*DWCN* 29-30)

His use of the term "foundations" in this passage is similar to his use of the multiple senses of the term "faith," in that foundations seem to be both "objectifiable systems" yet also "inescapable and inaccessible assumptions." The obvious response is to say that within the category of "inescapable interpretive assumptions" there will always be some which are objectifiable at a given point in time, and some which are not. The problem is that Fish's argument depends upon both a stability and flexibility in these categories. In spite of the insistence that these categories must be variable over time, his position implicitly depends upon certain kinds of assumptions (factual claims) always being accessible, while others must never be accessible (i.e., the criteria for "what constitutes what constitutes . . . etc." a factual claim). One question he leaves unanswered is, "How could foundations *always* be 'vulnerable to challenges from other localities and other times,' if the very possibility of challenging assumptions depends upon other assumptions being shared?" The possibility of inter-cultural challenge, therefore, depends upon some shared universal reality. Fish had earlier posited an essentialist vision of human identity by insisting that the universal deployment of interpretive strategies, in general, is constitutive of being human (*ITTC* 172). Such objections, however, would miss the point in two ways: first, the various inter-cultural challenges would not have to be based on the *same* set of shared interpretive assumptions in each case; second, the universal assertion of what constitutes human knowing is genuinely held as such, but with the knowledge that one could later become equally convinced of an opposing view.

The central (but unmentioned) element in the passage quoted above, which allows Fish to assert both the universal truth of his position and the contingency of that same belief, is the temporal quality of epistemic experience: the recognition that he cannot hold his beliefs as anything other than universally true, but that *in the future* he *may* hold a completely different set of beliefs as universally true, including that belief in the contingency of his own position. The irrefutability of such a view lies in the fact that it really does have no consequences, insofar as it amounts to saying nothing more than "people do what they do." However, as a position which denies itself the dignity of claiming consequences, it is also a truly dialectical or self-consuming presentation, because, like Augustine's *On Christian Doctrine,* the argument concludes by making itself superfluous (*SCA* 38), as it attempts to gesture towards that which cannot be contained within its discursive forms (i.e., inaccessible assumptions). In spite of the major changes between *Self-Consuming Artifacts* and *Doing What Comes Naturally,* the issue of our chronological experience of understanding has remained central in Fish's position: from the idea of "literature in the reader," to the concept of "dialectic" as a progressive revelation, to the question of how the assumptions of an interpretive community change over time. In this way, the idea of dialectic is still central to his position, not despite, but *because of* the rejection of the hope of formal truth.

The mention of dialectic leads to one further important difference between *Doing What Comes Naturally* and the works written before it. Earlier we noted the way in which Fish initially presents the idea of "dialectic" in *Self-Consuming Artifacts,* and then continues to develop and apply it in *Is There a Text in This Class?* Implicit within his characterization of "dialectical" or "self-consuming" presentations is a contrast between two views of epistemology: the "philosophical" (self-consuming/dialectical/anti-discursive) position and the "rhetorical" (self-satisfying/logical/discursive) position. In *Doing What Comes Naturally,* Fish describes the way rhetoric has traditionally been characterized: i.e., in opposition to the "philosophic tradition," which includes Milton and Plato (*DWCN* 471-73). The usual (philosophic) argument distinguishes rhetoric from truth and then shows how rhetoric can be used to persuade people without any reference to the truth (472). The indictment of rhetoric is then deduced from its ability to function as a technique without any "moral centre" (473). Fish proceeds from this characterization of rhetoric to present the common rhetorician's response (478-85), but the importance of his argument is that in making it, Fish repeats the debate, outlined above, between formalism and anti-formalism (477-78). In his attempt to draw parallels between the philosophic and formalist tradition, on the one hand, and the rhetorical and anti-formalist tradition on the other, Fish's description is the complete reverse of those categories that he uses in *Self-Consuming Artifacts.* In the earlier work he places Plato (as well as Milton and Augustine) on the side of the "anti-logical" dialecticians. Fish now links the practices of the rhetorician with anti-objectivist epistemology, whereas, in *Self-Consuming Artifacts,* the rhetorician's position was linked with objectivist epistemology. In the earlier work, the rhetoricians were identified (and implicitly indicted) as the rationalist/formalist philosophers of the Restoration (*SCA* 380-81); however, in the later work, Fish identifies himself as an anti-formalist rhetorician. This shift in categories is important, because it demonstrates the benefit of his earlier reading, in that it allows him to use the "dialectical" method of the philosopher to articulate and defend a rhetorician's argument.

In attempting to equate the debate between the rhetorical and philosophical positions with the debate between formalists and anti-formalists, Fish notes that we cannot attempt to decide between these two positions without adopting the assumptions of one side or the other (*DWCN* 483-84). In effect, an awareness of the debate can be predicated only upon the emergence of those assumptions which will simultaneously determine which side of the argument we will take. The problem is that in spite of Fish's declared anti-formalism, this very distinction is presented as a formalist dichotomy which is inescapable, like the true/false branches on a logic tree. As far as his own interpretation of that debate is concerned, Fish insists, "It is not my intention here to endorse either [the rhetorical or philosophic interpretation of] history or to offer a third or to argue as some have for a nonhistory of discontinuous *episteme* innocent of either a progressive or lapsarian curve; rather, I only wish to point out that the debate continues to this very day" (485). According to his own position, even as an attempt to "point out" the debate, his description cannot avoid interpreting the debate, and his interpretation must be from one side or the other of this very conflict which he insists is unavoidable. In this way, his argument attempts to lock all others into an inescapable and unresolvable formalist dichotomy, while adopting a position which implicitly transcends that same dichotomy.

It may seem that such an objection is yet another example of the same old strategy of finding contradictions within anti-formalism by beginning with the assumptions of formalist logic. In this case, however, it is Fish who introduces the totalizing formalist dichotomy between rhetoric and philosophy. Within his own account of the ongoing debate, Fish notes a possible third alternative in those who attempt to defend rhetoric by making it dependent upon truth and virtue (e.g., *"rem tene, verba sequentur"* or *"bene dicere non possit nisi bonus"*) (*DWCN* 473). The problem with such an approach, he argues, can be seen in Augustine's *On Christian Doctrine,* in that rhetoric effectively disappears within wisdom (473). In this respect, Fish's own ability to transcend the totalizing dichotomy that he describes depends, in effect, on inverting Augustine's argument so that wisdom is subsumed within rhetoric. However, if we recognize that Fish's account of the debate between philosophy and rhetoric must assume the truth of the rhetoricians' view, while we cannot fault his representation for being biased or unbiased (non-existent categories), we can be certain that an opposing interpretation would be equally unassailable on the same grounds. Hence, just as it is impossible to decide between competing interpretations by appealing to some illusory "text," reader-response theory (and the anti-foundationalism it leads to) does not need to be judged as true or false, because it self-destructs before any such judgment could be made. In effect, the wheels on the interpretive wagon are put back on before they could "theoretically" fall off, because interpretation has never stopped.

If the rhetorical/anti-formalist position is concerned exclusively with contextual constraints, rather than disembodied truth, how can Fish's anti-formalism deny having consequences but still justify itself within its own contextual requirement that it be applicable? Fish does not argue that all action has no consequences, but that each action/interpretation has consequences only within the spheres of influence of those inaccessible assumptions from which it emerges. Fish's specific contention is that anti-foundationalism does not have *the* consequences which others claim it has. The impossibility of ever being free from some constraints (faith assumptions) means that both the conservative fear of anarchy and the anti-establishment hopes for "freedom" are equally unfounded, because both are predicated upon the existence of a radically free individual (one fearing that freedom, the other desiring it) (*DWCN* 321-24). This is why Fish can conclude that although theory (formalist or anti-formalist) has no consequences, it will always appear to have consequences by virtue of the fact that it will always be in the process of reflecting political changes which have already occurred (321). However, this does not change the admittedly contextual fact that the presently universalized criteria for what constitutes justification require that a theory have consequences. This may be why Fish is willing to concede that "theory's day is dying; the hour is late; and the only thing left for a theorist to do is to say so, which is what I have been saying here, and, I think, not a moment too soon" (341).

In *There's No Such Thing as Free Speech* Fish continues his twofold offensive against both formalism and "inconsistent anti-formalism," specifically as they operate in the legal and political debates relating to the "culture wars."[2] His first step is to expose the pretensions to objectivity in the neo-conservative appropriation of the language of liberalism. Because liberalism makes a continually implicit claim to objective truth, it denies the availability of a transcendent perspective while employing its own universal claims (16-17). This is why Fish can argue against the very existence of liberalism (as an impossible claim to objectivity), and

41

state that "the structure of liberal thought is my target in every one of these essays" (16). Given that there is no realm of objective or unconstrained speech, there is no truly "free speech," because even if it did "exist," *per se*, it could not be made manifest in a temporal context where humans could experience it (113-17). In this respect, Fish is repeating the insistence that our ability to think is predicated upon value claims which we cannot completely objectify (117). It is not necessary here to describe the similar arguments Fish makes against several different aspects of the neo-conservative appropriation of the language of liberal neutrality within the "culture wars." It is more important to note that while making these arguments against the formalist appeals of conservatives, Fish is also arguing against the utopian aspirations of various liberal positions which are inconsistent in their anti-formalism. He brings this aspect of his argument into sharpest focus in analysing new historicist criticism. He points out that although all perceptions are grounded in historical assumptions, because such a claim is itself "metacritical" it can have no bearing on any specific historical claims (247-48). That is, historiography will be motivated and constrained by discipline-specific criteria, regardless of a person's metaphysical (or anti-metaphysical) beliefs about the possibility of universal truth. New historical criticism is no less bound by historical/contextual constraints (professional/academic) than those positions against which it reacts and is therefore equally incapable of effecting the political change for which its practitioners hope (249-51). From these arguments we can make two points regarding *There's No Such Thing as Free Speech:* first, his approach is still dependent upon his use of the multiple senses of "faith," as he continues to attack both formalism and inconsistent anti-formalism; second, his criticism of new historicist and liberal "theory hope" sounds exactly like the objections raised earlier against his own position.

Fish can indict others for inconsistent anti-foundationalism, but he can do so only to the extent that he claims consequences for his own position. In effect, being able to cite specific problems in a new historical reading, on the grounds that it falsely claims influence beyond the academy, is itself no less an extra-disciplinary or metacritical claim. If his own position is consistently anti-formalist, then it must, as such, avoid having the consequences of making even such context-specific normative claims. Therefore, Fish can only indict other partial anti-formalist positions to the same extent that he is inconsistent with his own inconsequential anti-formalism. If, on the other hand, we allow such normative claims on the qualification that Fish gives for his own anti-

formalism—that is, we are incapable of holding our own views as anything other than universally true for the time being—then we must
grant the same qualification to other versions of anti-formalism.
Therefore, either the category of "inconsistent anti-formalism" includes
his own position (creating a contradiction), or it includes only those
anti-formalist positions which do not share Fish's politics. If we grant
the second alternative, then his indictment of other positions (whether
new historicist or neo-conservative) amounts to nothing more than the
discovery/non-discovery of "biases"—a strategy which he has already
dismissed. Fish is, of course, aware of the problem.

The primary way in which he alleviates this tension, within *There's No
Such Thing as Free Speech,* is through an explicit return to the discourse
of "faith." In examining his other works thus far, we have seen how Fish
makes his own reader-response theory (and anti-formalism in general)
into a self-consuming artifact which demonstrates its own irrelevance.
His reading of Augustine provides him with a dialectical method which
eventually allows him to "transcend" the assumptions upon which his
notion of "dialectic" depends. This development, in conjunction with
his anti-rationalist reading of the *Phaedrus,* allows him to incarnate the
dialectical method in his own writing without necessarily implying the
existence of a metaphysical truth, towards which such a presentation
normally gestures. As a result, Fish is able to use the method of the
philosopher to defend his position as a rhetorician. The only universal
realities which Fish consistently endorses are those inescapable yet inaccessible interpretive assumptions which cannot be specified. The ability of these vacuous deities to be both omnipresent and nowhere present is derived from the operation of two kinds of "faith," to which Fish
also allows a quasi-substantive status. He uses "faith" to refer to both an
objectifiable interpretive system and a set of inaccessible assumptions,
but he also uses it in that third sense, to describe the only basis for
accepting the existence of those inaccessible and inescapable assumptions. This third appeal to "faith" allows Fish to escape momentarily the
usual contextual constraints regarding "what constitutes evidence" etc.
In this way, his use of the stance of "faith" (as with dialectic) allows him
to avoid foundationalism while simultaneously benefiting from the
notions of objective truth which are continually implicit within it.

The attraction of Fish's argument is in the sophisticated pragmatism
it offers: it allows him to demonstrate not only that the abandonment
of metaphysics does not, indeed cannot, lead to relativism or nihilism,
but that our inescapable contextual constraints entail that our metaphysical or anti-metaphysical beliefs have no consequences at all. The

argument attempts to transcend the foundationalist/anti-foundationalist debate by employing the stance of faith, but his own logic requires that he must not be able to distinguish between various objects of faith. Because "faith" cannot avoid having an object, the subtle shifts between verbal and substantive uses of the term, in reaching this conclusion, still leave us with the question, "Faith in what?"

In the remaining chapters we shall attempt to answer this question, by examining in more detail how Fish manages to extricate his general argument for the primacy of interpretive assumptions from any dependence upon the specific content of his reading of Augustine. However, before proceeding, we shall look at a couple of instances where Fish makes his own claims about the nature of "faith." These comments help to explain the approach that I shall be taking in the remaining chapters. Fish presents one of his most explicit treatments of "faith" in an interview, entitled "The Contemporary Sophist," which is appended to *There's No Such Thing as Free Speech.* Here Fish describes the one exam that he gave in every course when he first began teaching:

> I asked the students to relate two sentences to each other and to the materials in the course. The first sentence was from J. Robert Oppenheimer: "Style is the deference that action pays to uncertainty." I took that to mean that in a world without certain foundations for action you avoid the Scylla of prideful self-assertion, on the one hand, and the Charybdis of paralysis, on the other hand, by stepping out provisionally, with a sense of style. The other quotation, which I matched and asked the students to consider, is from the first verse of Hebrews Eleven: "Now faith is the substance of things hoped for, the evidence of things not seen." I take that to be the classically theological version of Oppenheimer's statement, and so the question of the relationship between style and faith, or between interpretation and action and certainty, has been the obsessive concern of my thinking since the first time I gave this test back in 1962 or 1963. I think there is nothing in my work that cannot be generated from these two assertions and their interactions. . . . Of course the quotation from Hebrews Eleven came in from my Milton work. (*NSFS* 293)

In this passage, "faith" is constituted by the attempt to find a balance between the immobility of epistemic uncertainty and the sin of presumption (pride). Because his use of the term here emphasizes the existential sense of faith as "trust," it corresponds most closely to that third meaning of "faith" to which Fish appeals, when he asks us to "believe" in the existence of inaccessible interpretive principles (*ITTC* 169); however, as a definition it gives rise to a number of questions. Why should we accept the ethical imperatives of humility and hope, upon which his notion of faith depends? Should those imperatives be offered as articles of faith them-

44

selves? How can we begin to answer these or similar questions without attempting to provide "reasons" for his faith, thereby making it something other than (unqualifiable) faith? If we temporarily set aside these questions, we can attend to the important way the above passage directly parallels Fish's earlier treatment of Augustine in *Self-Consuming Artifacts*. In describing the self-consuming conclusion to Augustine's *On Christian Doctrine*, Fish points out that the superfluity of the speaker/preacher implies a need for balance:

> Obviously such an obligation imposes a great many difficulties, not the least of which is avoiding the Scylla and Charybdis of pride and despair. (*SCA* 40)

Although this statement and the one above are separated by over twenty years, together they suggest that this particular idea of "faith," which arguably "generated" most of his work, is taken from his reading of Augustine. We are also reminded of this influence when Fish cites Hebrews 11 in discussing Augustine's pivotal distinction between "use" and "enjoyment" (*SCA* 24). It therefore seems that Fish's reading of Augustine has had a formative influence upon his thinking — until we remember that, by his own account, Fish takes his interpretation of Hebrews 11 and the accompanying notion of "faith," not from Augustine but from his reading of Milton, which he then consciously brings to his reading of Augustine's *On Christian Doctrine*. Although none of these parallels provide conclusive evidence, they raise a question which the next chapter will attempt to answer: To what extent is Fish's reading of Augustine dictated by the assumptions introduced by reading as a Miltonist?

We can begin to see the relevance of this question, if we remember that Fish takes Milton to be (in some sense) an anti-foundationalist, and argues that Milton's antinomianism, which rejects the Ten Commandments as a standard for "good works" in favor of "faith," takes him "far down the anti-foundationalist road" (*NSFS* 292). Fish sees Milton's idea of radical dependence upon the Holy Spirit and "faith" as similar to postmodern rejection of objective truth (292). Even if we grant Fish's reading of Milton, it does not necessarily demonstrate the inevitability of anti-formalism, as much as it shows that, within Milton's work, Neoplatonic rationalism provides a sufficient basis for moving from foundationalism to anti-foundationalism. We shall attempt, therefore, to discern whether Fish's own work mirrors that same development in such a way that his anti-foundationalism is predicated only upon the tacit deployment of foundationalist epistemology. We shall also attempt to determine whether we can find alternatives to the foundationalist/anti-foundationalist dichotomy, if we avoid reading Augustine's work through a "Miltonic" lens. The obvious question, given our preceding discussion of interpretive principles, is what "lens" I will be using to read Augustine. The correspondingly obvious response, according to Fish's argument, is, "I cannot say, and neither can you. To the very extent that you (as a reader) understand what I have written, the relevant inaccessible and inescapable interpretive assumptions are no less inaccessible to you." This, as expected, leaves us where we started. Recognizing our own inescapable immediate context, the present reading will operate from an admittedly contemporary perspective which attempts to be Augustinian, rather than an admittedly contemporary perspective which is Miltonic in its attempt to be Augustinian. However, the present argument does not attempt to prove "biographically" why Fish employs the assumptions that he does. In that respect, the argument might easily be reversed, given that Fish was a medievalist before he became a Miltonist (*NSFS* 269). Instead, we shall ask simply whether Fish's attempt to apply his reading of Augustine to debates over seventeenth-century literature has already brought the foundationalist/anti-foundationalist dichotomy into his interpretive assumptions.

CHAPTER THREE

Charity

Before examining in more detail how Fish's idea of anti-foundationalist "faith" shapes his reading of Augustine, we need to make three important qualifications. The first concerns the terminology of our discussion. In his introduction to *Doing What Comes Naturally,* Fish admits, and attempts to qualify, the "(relative) crudeness" of the way in which his arguments employ "a number of key terms that are invoked as if they were monolithic and unproblematical" (*DWCN* 30). Because he tends to group "foundationalism," "rationalism" and "formalism," he can then equate "anti-foundationalism" with "anti-formalism," as well as "rhetoric," and use them almost interchangeably. Although I shall avoid forcing a refinement of these terms onto Fish's arguments, only to use them as a grounds for indictment, it is necessary to clarify my own use of some of these terms. The broadest of these categories is "rationalism," which will be used here to indicate the belief that the human ability to reason constitutes the primary faculty of human knowing. "Foundationalism" can then be understood as a category within rationalism, which indicates the predominantly modern tendency to seek for self-evident first principles upon which certain knowledge can then be constructed logically. "Formalism," in the broadest sense, is also usually a type of rationalism, involving the specific assertion that truth consists of a mind-independent reality, which may be material or ideal. Because of the obvious potential for overlap between these terms, Fish is justified in grouping them together as a unified "objectivist" opposition to his arguments.

A second qualification needs to be made regarding Fish's view that any attempt to observe interpretive influences or premises (in this case his) amounts to a non-action because assumptions of some kind are always inescapable. We are interested in more than simply "observing biases," because any assumptions that we could access, in relation to understanding his argument, would necessarily be mutually accessible. Instead, because we are operating within a discursive context that we share with Fish—as readers of Milton and/or Augustine—we can argue that there is a better way to read. More importantly, our ability to judge a "better" reading will depend, not upon a tacitly employed notion of "value," but on an explicit (but necessarily general) recognition that "better" will ultimately be judged by mutually inaccessible shared assumptions.

Thirdly, it would be dishonest if I were to suggest that my own reading of Augustine is not deeply influenced by Fish's thinking. Even as I take issue with certain aspects of his interpretation of Augustine, my own reading will be shaped as a response to his position. There are, however, alternatives to the usual postmodern platitudes about the mutually dependent nature of all oppositional strategies. There is an even deeper sense in which I recognize that Fish's arguments enable me to read Augustine in way that I could not otherwise. This is why, in the midst of disagreement, there is not only opposition, but gratitude. One alternative approach to the issue of mutually dependent oppositional strategies is to ask how such constraints could be so unrelenting, if they are really only contingent. How can we think the supplementarity of all difference to be necessary, if at that moment we are questioning whether supplementarity and necessity can have any relation at all? Given this uncertainty, rather than argue against either position, I shall attempt simply to delineate how Fish's arguments change, as they are brought into a more consistent engagement of Augustine's position. In this way, we can begin to encounter anew some of the persistent implications of Augustine's writings.

In his Introduction to *Doing What Comes Naturally,* Fish outlines the "steps" involved in going "down the anti-formalist road" (25-26). As Fish himself observes, these "stages" are not so much "steps," as they are implications, which are all included within the attempt to locate meaning in intention rather than in formal structures (25). Once intention (authorial or otherwise) is admitted as the source of meaning, we cannot escape the need to "interpretively establish" that intention, and thereby base our knowledge of that intention upon persuasion (25). Given the centrality of persuasion, we are then led to the conclusion that both the facts we perceive and the interpretive assumptions by which we constitute them are determined by contextual constraints (25-26). Although such an argument is, by now, expected from Fish, the most revealing part of his summary is the parenthetical remark concerning our inability to avoid going "the rest of the way" down the anti-formalist path, once we have taken that first step: "this insight is writ large in the history of Reformation theology" (26). Although there are numerous points of historical debate at which one could take issue with such a broad generalization, Fish's comment is presently more important to us because of what it indicates about the

48

influence of Milton upon his own view of the Reformation. Given that Fish is a Miltonist, it is not at all surprising that he should draw his examples of Protestant interpretive development from Milton's prose. We are not concerned here to challenge Fish's repeated insistence that Protestant hermeneutics took Milton "rather far down the anti-foundationalist road" (*NSFS* 292-93; see also *DWCN* 8-9). However, Fish never mentions that the anti-formalist ethics he finds in Milton's *Christian Doctrine* (*NSFS* 292) are themselves predicated upon a foundationalist epistemology.[1] Our first task is to discern the extent to which the interpretive strategies of the theological tract are guided by the assumptions of rationalist epistemology. The second step will focus on how Fish uses that epistemology mistakenly to characterize the "logocentric" tradition. We can then return to Augustine's *On Christian Doctrine,* in order to determine how Fish's reading of Augustine is shaped by foundationalist assumptions.

In *There's No Such Thing as Free Speech,* Fish focuses on the second part of Milton's *Christian Doctrine* as an illustration of how the location of meaning in intention leads to anti-foundationalism. Book 2 of Milton's treatise is concerned with the question, "What is a good work?" Fish points out that by defining a good work as "one that is informed by the working of the Holy Spirit in you," Milton makes it impossible to identify a "good work" objectively (*CD* 638; *NSFS* 292). As conclusive proof for this position, Fish cites Milton's insistence that "faith" rather than the Ten Commandments is the basis for Christian ethics (292). Fish concludes:

> Now, if within two or three paragraphs of your discussion of ethics, which is what the second book of *The Christian Doctrine* is, you have dislodged the ten commandments as the repository of ethical obligation, you are rather far down the anti-foundationalist road. And Milton is a strong antinomian, by which I mean he refuses to flinch in the face of the extraordinary existential anxiety produced by antinomianism. (*NSFS* 292)

Once again, the validity of Fish's reading depends upon his use of the term "faith." The problem with Fish's interpretation is that Milton has already stated what he means by the "faith" which is to replace the Ten Commandments. At the beginning of both book 1 and book 2 of his treatise Milton repeats the twofold division of the work:

> The PARTS of CHRISTIAN DOCTRINE are two: FAITH, or KNOWLEDGE OF GOD, and LOVE, or THE WORSHIP OF GOD. (*CD* 128)

> The first book dealt with FAITH and THE KNOWLEDGE OF GOD. This second book is about THE WORSHIP OF GOD and CHARITY. (637)

The topics of "faith" and "love" are understandably commonplace throughout the history of Christian theology; however, because Milton's definition of terms equates "faith" with "knowledge of God," he makes "charity" or "worship of God" dependent upon his epistemology. By the force of his definitions, because "good works" are constituted by "faith," "charity" is dependent upon "knowledge of God." To some extent, this much is also commonplace. Although the pivotal question is how Milton then defines "knowledge of God," we can already see that, when Milton states that good works must be those which are done "through true faith" (*CD* 638), he means "through believing things that are true about God." Milton's ethical system is predicated, therefore, not upon an existential or subjectivist notion of "faith," but upon our need to believe the "true theology" which he has just finished outlining in book 1.

If we look briefly at book 1 of *Christian Doctrine*, we can begin to see the extent to which Milton's idea of "the knowledge of God" (i.e., faith) depends upon foundationalist epistemology. Such a claim may initially seem both surprising and unsupportable, given that Milton explicitly disavows human reason (132-33) and philosophy (127) as sources of knowledge concerning God, opting instead for *sola scriptura:*

> We must, then, look for this doctrine not among philosophizing academics, and not among the laws of men, but in the Holy Scriptures alone with the Holy Spirit as guide. (127)

In a similar manner, Milton notes the inability of "reason alone" to discern anything more than God's existence (132-33). In these and similar statements, Milton seems to be making a sharp distinction between reason and revelation in order to place himself (and his treatise) firmly on the side of revelation. However, "the philosophizing academics" that he so strongly opposes are specifically the scholastics. Similarly, his warnings against using reason to discern the attributes of God are part of his later argument against the scholastic "sophistry" used to explain the Trinity (212). One of Milton's central (and more contentious) points in *Christian Doctrine* is his argument against the Trinity. We are not concerned here with his argument as such, but throughout the treatise he consistently associates the doctrine of the Trinity with the legacy of the irrational scholastic metaphysics of "Papist" philosophers (203-04, 212, 421-24). He seems to think that the Trinity, once viewed rationally, will be rejected by all clear-thinking Protestants, just as they rejected the doctrine of transubstantiation. Milton's explicit rejections of "philosophizing" and "reason alone" are best understood, therefore, not as a pretence to disavow the inescapable role of human thought, but as part of his specific argument against the Trinity. How then does Milton employ reason? If we look at Milton's stated approach to Scripture, and at the operation of rationalist categories in his theological arguments, we can see that *Christian Doctrine* is informed by a foundationalist epistemology.

Initially, Milton seems to take his interpretive starting points from the commonplace Reformation dicta of *sola fide* and *sola scriptura*. However, as we have already noted, he effectively reduces the former to the latter, by making knowledge of true doctrine derived from Scripture both the object of "faith" (in the verbal sense) (*CD* 129), and the content of "faith" (in the substantive sense) (638-40). What is more important for present purposes is the way that Milton draws different implications from both of these two Reformation dicta:

> But in fact, I decided not to depend upon the belief or the judgment of others in religious questions for this reason: God has revealed the way of eternal salvation only to the individual faith of each man and demands of us that any man who wishes to be saved should work out his beliefs for himself. So I made up my mind to puzzle out a religious creed for myself by my own exertions, and to acquaint myself with it thoroughly. In this the only authority I accepted was God's self-revelation, and accordingly I read and pondered the Holy Scriptures themselves with all possible diligence never sparing myself in any way. (118)

In one sense, these statements from the Prefatory Epistle show that Milton is simply taking the Reformation theological project on its own terms (individual faith and Scripture) and attempting to make it more rigorously consistent with those principles. The first word in the above passage, translated as "but," is the word "verum" in the Latin text (*DDC*, IM 5). This emphatic connective term links the present passage with the immediately preceding disavowal of all political or public motivation for his treatise (*CD* 118), thereby emphasizing the individual orientation of his query. Contrary to Regina Schwartz, who sees a problematic tension in the above passage between Milton's authority and that of Scripture (Schwartz 229-30), Milton is simply taking the scriptural imperative for individual faith to its logical extreme. The problem is that the emphasis upon individual faith leads to a strong emphasis upon the specifically isolated individual:

> I pursued my studies and so far satisfied myself that eventually I had no doubt about my ability to distinguish correctly in religion between matters of faith and matters of opinion. It was, furthermore, my greatest comfort that I had constructed, with God's help, a powerful support for my faith. (*CD* 121)

51

Milton is able to contrast "faith" with "opinion," specifically because he defines "faith" as "knowledge of God." Several implications follow from this passage: first, Milton's own mind operating in isolation is the only judge in estimating his "ability to distinguish correctly" (there is no reference to any consultation with a community of believers); second, Milton is specifically looking for knowledge which is beyond doubt (a quest for "certainty" that can be justifiably contrasted with "opinion"); third, that certainty provides a basis upon which he can "construct" a "powerful support" for his knowledge of God ("faith"). Milton's self-proclaimed approach to Scripture is, therefore, a radically individual quest for certainty which provides a basis for his knowledge. The individualism is slightly restrained, or qualified, by the phrase "with God's help"; however, as a parenthetical adverbial phrase it does not substantially alter the main action of the statement. Even if the second instance of the term "faith," in the above passage, is taken to mean the action of "trust," rather than a constituted system of belief, the statement still makes his epistemic "construct" the object of his faith. In effect Milton's faith "rests" on his own ability to judge between "faith" (true knowledge) and "opinion." Although these passages from the Prefatory Epistle do not prove that Milton's theological arguments depend upon foundationalist epistemology, they demonstrate that Milton conflates the Reformation dicta of *sola fide* and *sola scriptura* with the rationalist epistemic criteria of *solus ego* and *sola indubitata*.

As noted earlier, we are not concerned here with the validity of Milton's argument against the Trinity *per se*, but if we look briefly at his argument we can see the central role played in it by rationalist categories. Milton insists that it is illogical to hold that three "persons" can form one "being" (212). This assertion depends upon his two earlier definitions: a "person" is an "individual thing gifted with intelligence"; a "substance" (or "essence") is only an abstraction from such an intelligent "thing itself" (142). The idea of human identity as a "thinking thing" (*res cogitans*) is a central element in the foundationalist project of Cartesian rationalist epistemology:

Here I find: it is cogitation; this alone cannot be rent from me. I am, I exist; it is certain. But for how long? So long as I am a cogitating thing, of course. For it could perhaps also happen that if I would cease all cogitation I as a whole would cease to be. I am now admitting nothing except what is necessarily true. I am, then, precisely only a cogitating thing [*res cogitans*], that is, a mind, or animus, or intellect, or reason: words with significations previously unknown to me. But I am a true thing, and truly existing. Yet what kind of thing? A thinking thing [*cogitans*], I have said. (Descartes 2.6; Heffernan trans.)

Two important elements within this passage bear directly on our discussion of Milton's *Christian Doctrine:* first, the passage presents the same vision of human identity, as a *res cogitans;* second, that formulation of human identity develops out of a similar quest for certainty ("method of doubt": Descartes 2.8-9), conducted by the self in isolation. It could be argued that in using such a formulation of human identity Milton is simply employing the very common and ancient idea that what distinguishes humans from other animals is the rational capacity (e.g., Aristotle 1098a5-10). However, Milton knows that his definition of "person" will be applied specifically to non-humans (that is, God). He also states that his definition is a "more recent use" of the term (*CD* 140-41). More importantly, the claim that reason is the distinctive and highest quality of human beings is not the same as the claim that personal identity consists solely of rational intellect. The latter position makes reason the exclusive essence of personal identity in a way that the former does not; that is, the former does not necessarily exclude the affections from personal identity. This point does not imply that the position of either Milton or Descartes is so reductive as simply to omit any and all consideration of the emotions or the will. Nor does it imply that Milton is a dualist. The relevant point is that epistemic primacy for Descartes lies in the reason, independent of other aspects of human existence (that is, he may or may not account for them, but they are are not basic to knowledge). More importantly, Milton employs this same rationalist formulation of the knowing subject, in establishing the premises which he will later use for his main argument against the Trinity.

Even if we grant the general influence of rationalist criteria upon Milton's approach to Scripture and upon a specific part of his argument against the Trinity, we have yet to see how foundationalist epistemology supports his theological project as a whole. The degree of influence becomes clear only if we consider first the relationship between Milton's *Artis Logicae Plenior Institutio* and Ramist "dialectic" in general, and then the relationship between his logic text and *De Doctrina Christiana.*

Milton views the Scholastics as the source of the trinitarian error, because of their confusion of logic with false metaphysics (*AL* 211). He patterned his *Artis Logicae* after the *Scholae Dialecticae* of Peter Ramus, because he recognized Ramus as part of a wider attempt to "purge" logic of such Scholastic superstition. The career of Peter Ramus could be characterized as an attempt to attack the strongholds of Aristotelian (Scholastic) logic (Copenhaver and Schmitt 230-39), given his view that Plato was superior to Aristotle (233). However, despite his alleged enthusiasm for Platonic "dialectic," Ramus's approach to Platonism differed significantly from those before him. The reductive quality of his approach is epitomized in his *Remarks on Aristotle:* "The foundations of arts are definitions, divisions or certain and sure inferences from definitions and divisions; there is nothing else" (quoted in C&S 234). Consequently, the main development effected by Ramist dialectic was the complete separation of reason from ethical considerations (C&S 237; cf. Ong, *Ramus* 8-9). Reason could then be viewed entirely as technique or *ars* (*techne*) (cf. Ong, *Rhetoric* 5-6). Another major aspect of Ramist logic was the extensive use of "bifurcating tables," which provided a clear, visual and spatial ordering of all the "topics" or "places" for a given discipline (C&S 230-31, 237-38). Because of the way that Ramus emphasized the Socratic analogy between dialectic and the *ars* (*techne*) of the physician (C&S 234), Milton is consistent with Ramist principles in naming his work *Artis Logicae Plenior Institutio.*

Milton does not use a Ramist "bifurcating table," as such, to display the topics or "places" of his *De Doctrina,* but the systematic division of his entire treatise into ever further nested subdivisions directly corresponds to the same principles of topical division and could be mapped onto such a table. Milton makes no attempt to hide the influence of Ramist logic upon the very form of his *De Doctrina,* and makes specific reference to the theological application of such logic within the Preface to *Artis Logicae:*

> For theologians produce rules about God, about divine substances, and about sacraments right out of the middle of logic as though these rules had been provided for their own use, although nothing is more foreign to logic, or indeed to logic itself, than the grounds for these rules as formulated by them. (*AL* 211)

This passage is notable as the only digression within the entire Preface from the immediate topic of introducing logic and the "arts," and raises the question of whether Milton might have published the *Artis Logicae* specifically as part of a larger educational and theological project. Although we will later examine one specific instance of the theological implications of this approach to Scripture, it is already clear that Milton saw an obvious connection between his *Artis Logicae* and his *De Doctrina Christiana.*

Even the name that Milton gives to his *Artis Logicae* (as opposed to *Scholae Dialecticae*) indicates his understanding of those changes that Ramus had effected by transforming ancient dialectic into modern logic. The title reflects what would become the radically modern understanding of the relation between making (*ars*) and knowing: knowledge as making, and knowledge solely for application (*ars logicae; techne-logos*) (Grant 12-20; cf.Strauss 88). In his Preface, Milton makes these same connections explicit:

> In the same way, the meaning of [the term] art is distinguished: when it signifies a teaching (*doctrina*), about which we are especially concerned here, it is the orderly assemblage of precepts and examples, or the method (*methodus*), by which anything is usefully taught. (*AL* 212)

In this passage we find both aspects of the modern foundationalist project fully operative. The logical arrangement of precepts makes "doctrine" an "art" (a "making"—*techne*, technique) and the purpose of the art is to teach something "usefully" (for application, making, further ordering). According to Milton's own terms, his *De Doctrina*, as an application of the *Artis Logicae*, is then purposely engaged in the "making" (ordering) of knowledge (doctrine) in such a way that it can be applied.

Earlier I noted that one of the specific ways in which Milton applies his logic is in his arguments against the Trinity. Gordon Campbell has claimed that "the philosophical arguments which Milton uses to deny these attributes [of God] to the Son were not formulated to shore up a specific theological point, but were drawn from his *Artis Logicae*" ("Son of God" 507). But to phrase the issue in this way overlooks the more plausible explanation (recently adopted by Campbell) that part of Milton's purpose in publishing the *Artis Logicae* in 1672—though not necessarily when composing it in the 1640s—could have been to support a larger theological project.[2] At the same time, Milton is able to use Ramist logic as a tool without contradicting his own disavowal of "philosophizing," because he views it as an effectively transparent medium, through which he can perceive the truth of Scripture. I am not, at this point, challenging Fish's general assertion that Milton's position eventually leads him to some anti-formalist conclusions. However, by looking more closely at how Milton begins and conducts his treatment of Scripture, we can see that his anti-formalist conclusions are made possible only because of his foundationalist assumptions.[3] Nor is the present argument an attempt to characterize Milton's wide-ranging, and more general, invocation of the "principle of reason." There are other important ways in which Milton seems directly opposed to the modern instrumental view of reason (e.g., associating *recta ratio* with knowledge of universal moral standards [*CD* 132]), but I am not trying here to characterize Milton's general view of reason (probably best described as vaguely "Platonic"). Rather, I am pointing out the foundationalist elements in the *De Doctrina* which Fish's argument might lead us to overlook by focusing upon the anti-formalism in Milton's ethical conclusions.

The primary difficulty in *De Doctrina*'s position results from taking the principle of *sola scriptura* to its logical extreme in such a way that the logic arguably violates Scripture. As testified by the industry in patristic studies among Renaissance Reformers, few theologians studied literally "Scripture alone." Instead, most Reformers used Scripture as the final authority in adjudicating between conflicting positions within that tradition of which they were a part (e.g., Luther eagerly anticipated the latest edition of St. Jerome's *Works*, edited by Erasmus [Vessey 69]). Milton is therefore exceptional among Reformers in that he insists upon such a radical deployment of the *sola scriptura* principle. What we find, however, is that while his extreme view of *sola scriptura* results from his foundationalist approach, the resulting interpretation leads to anti-foundationalist conclusions. We do not have the opportunity here to explore this dynamic tension throughout the *De Doctrina*; however, we can find this very same process, "writ small," as it were, in Milton's second antiprelatical tract. Fish presents his own reading of this tract in an essay entitled, "Wanting a Supplement: The Question of Interpretation in Milton's Early Prose."

If we examine Fish's reading of Milton's *Of Prelaticall Episcopacy*, we can see that although Fish may be accurate in delineating poststructuralist tendencies within the tract, he does so in such a way that conceals the foundationalist assumptions that give shape to Milton's *sola scriptura* approach. Fish's primary argument in "Wanting a Supplement" focuses upon the way that Milton attempts to "argue" for the self-sufficency of Scripture without contradicting himself in the very act of presenting such an argument ("Wanting" 42-44). As Fish explains, the idea of Scripture as "self-sufficent" means that any external supplement to the text is both "unnecessary and dangerous; it is unnecessary because the Scripture is by definition sufficient and complete in and of itself, and it is dangerous because as something added, a supplement may come to stand in place of, even overwhelm, that which it is brought in to assist" (41-42). The obvious question is, if Scripture really is self-sufficient, how can it be threatened by that from which it is supposedly independent? Or, conversely, why does it continually require interpretation (defense) of precisely the sort that Milton is undertaking? In effect, if Scripture is self-sufficient, why does Milton need to write his tract? At the same time, if his tract presents a successful argument, how can he keep his own argument from becoming a basis for his faith in Scripture, thereby replacing that which it attempts to defend? Fish uses this tension over scriptural self-sufficiency to draw a parallel between Milton's tract and the Derridean notion of "supplementarity" (42-43). Fish is, however, quick to qualify the deconstructive parallel:

> I do not mean to suggest that Milton is a proto-poststructuralist; rather I mean to suggest that in the context of the position he self-consciously espouses, he is inevitably aware of the difficulties and "troubles" on which post-structuralism feeds.
>
> My thesis, then, is that Milton, no less than his modern deconstructive reader, is uneasy about his performance, and for similar reasons. In a word, that performance is superfluous, and because it is superfluous, it is also, potentially at least, impious. (44)

Because Milton is aware of this tension within his own work, he must continually attempt to present a "non-argument argument":

> Needless to say, this is a difficult strategy to execute since it is always in danger of turning into the very thing it opposes, of turning into a supplement. (46)

And therefore:

> [Milton] doesn't *discredit* the evidence; he discredits the possibility of either discrediting or crediting the evidence, and thereby saves himself both the labor and the possible presumption that would inhere in even the slightest of [such] actions. (47)

The mention of "presumption" reminds us why this reading might sound familiar. In another context this tract would be called a "self-consuming artifact," which simultaneously attempts to avoid "the Scylla and Charybdis of pride and despair" (*SCA* 40). However, as we have seen, in yet another context, Fish explicitly adopts this same principle of balance as his own, when he equates Hebrews 11:1 with a quotation from Oppenheimer:

> I took that [Oppenheimer quotation] to mean that in a world without certain foundations for action you avoid the Scylla of prideful self-assertion, on the one hand, and the Charybdis of paralysis on the other. (*NSFS* 293)

In *Of Prelaticall Episcopacy*, Milton effectively opts for the "paralysis" extreme. He does this by systematically introducing the arguments of apostolic or patristic authorities only to dismiss them before their evidence can be heard, because to admit them would be to supplement Scripture ("Wanting" 48-51). In effect, the tract attempts to say nothing.

In the second half of "Wanting a Supplement," Fish goes on to show how Milton takes his interpretive approach to the opposite extreme in the *Doctrine and Discipline of Divorce,* where he actively engages in supplementing Scripture. Written only two years after *Of Prelaticall Episcopacy,* the divorce tract no longer forbids the interpretation, or supplementing, of Scripture, but actually commands it ("Wanting" 53-54). In effect, Milton engages in precisely that kind of activity which the other tract denounced as so dangerous. He proceeds to interpret a passage of Scripture in such a way that the "intended" meaning of the prohibition against divorce (Matt. 7:19) is precisely the opposite of what the "plain sense" would seem initially to indicate (54-56). The key point of Fish's argument is that Milton goes "down the anti-formalist road" by locating meaning in intention (56-57). Fish demonstrates that Milton effectively re-contextualizes the verse in such a way that, by the time he returns to the verse prohibiting divorce, the "obvious" reading of the verse is precisely the opposite of what it "obviously" meant before. Of course, the "verse" as a formal reality has now disappeared within Fish's reading (though not within Milton's), because its meaning is only a function of the interpretive or contextual constraints in which it becomes embedded. Milton would obviously insist that his context is the correct one, but such a conclusion is precisely what Fish will not allow:

> What Milton wants is at once to put the force of interpretation into play and to arrest that play the moment it produces the configuration he desires. ("Wanting" 61)

Although Fish is very careful to make allowance for Milton's own contextual constraints, his reading of the *Doctrine and Discipline of Divorce* is unable to avoid implicitly indicting Milton for being too "presumptuous" (the other interpretive extreme). He then explains the tension within Milton's writing, between the anti-formalism, which initiates interpretive play, and the formalism which tries to arrest it. Fish maintains that Milton "still deeply feared and resisted the dissolution of the ego" (Aers & Hodge 19, as quoted in "Wanting" 66). The problem is that in one sense Milton wants "to dissolve his ego, and he wants to be the one (the ego) that announces and performs the dissolving" (66). What is most revealing about Fish's position, however, is the way he proceeds to generalize from his reading of Milton to all human experience:

> "Who can think submission?" asks Satan (*PL* 1.661), a question that is precise in its articulation of a requirement that cannot be met. One can think about submission all day long, but with every thought submission will once

again be deferred; it is simply not possible to affirm the diacritical nature of one's being without betraying that affirmation in the very act of producing it. ("Wanting" 66)

In effect, Milton's (Satan's) problem is everyone's problem, according to Fish, because just as no one can actually live as though there is no universal truth (poststructuralism must continually betray itself), it is impossible to submit (or be "truly humble") by trying to do so consciously or with understanding. We shall examine the validity and implications of this position in more detail later, but at this point we must note a number of immediately obvious ways in which this generalization creates problems for itself. First, although it is perfectly natural to distinguish the action of submitting from the action of thinking about submitting, such a distinction does not make either activity inherently impossible. For example, it may be that hoping is not the same as thinking about hoping, but that does not imply that we are never capable of hoping. Second, by insisting that conscious submission is impossible, Fish inadvertently implies his own supplement-free category: "false humility." His basic argument seems to be as follows: true humility requires an absence of self-awareness; self-awareness is inescapable insofar as anyone "attempts" to be humble; therefore, humility is impossible for anyone consciously trying to be humble. Because all "attempts" at humility are necessarily false, the term "false humility" is able to operate as a category without the existence of real humility. Third, the most deeply rooted problem in Fish's generalization is the assertion (operative in many of his arguments) that objectivist epistemology of all kinds always involves egoism and pride, whereas anti-formalism is at least an attempt, insofar as possible/impossible, not to avoid the unavoidable false humility (*amor fati*).[4]

The inescapable nature of egoism is important for Fish's argument, not only for the continuity that he sees between these two radically different tracts by Milton, but also for the basis of Fish's own characterization of "logocentrism." In attempting to explain how Milton could write such directly opposed tracts within two years of each other, Fish points out that, aside from the obvious changes in his domestic situation, Milton is still consistent in his appeal to the "conscience" of the individual ("Wanting" 54). This appeal leads to an emphasis upon interpretation, which allows Milton to employ the notion of the "plain sense" of Scripture in two distinct and opposing ways. Those who oppose Milton's reading of Mathew 7:19 are indicted for seeing only the "plain sense," in that their reading is deemed carnal, legalistic or superficial, while Milton's own reading is claimed as "most evident," because he is able to "discover plainly" the truly obvious context of the verse (56). What Fish never states is that Milton's emphasis upon individual "conscience" is nothing more than the rationalist ego holding Scripture before it as an object of mastery. Both the formalist and anti-formalist Miltonic positions that Fish describes are dependent upon the assumption that Scripture is primarily a reified object, a book of multivalent cipher which can be operated like any other system. Because the operative sense of "intention" in both cases assumes a mastering subject, the anti-formalist position, which develops out of locating meaning in intention, is no less dependent than the formalist position upon the belief in a stable subject and object. Milton's version of *sola scriptura* necessarily implodes because of the reductive rationality that underlies his hermeneutic. The "Scripture" that he is afraid of supplementing in the first tract is only the objectifiable physical text. This radically formalist view of Scripture is what then leads to the impossibility of formal truth.

This same supplementarity operates in Fish's more general characterization of the "logocentric" tradition. Borrowing from the lexicon of Derridean deconstruction, Fish characterizes the logocentric tradition as that which privileges the notions of the interior, breathed, spiritual or intentional over the external, written, carnal or literal ("Wanting" 42). It is this tradition which abhors or fears "that dangerous supplement" (42). Initially Fish maintains that this logocentric fear of the supplement is part of a formalist belief in objective truth (43), but then he goes on to argue that the insistence upon intention (i.e., spirit) is actually the source of an anti-formalism which is unable to objectify truth (57). The primary difficulty in Fish's argument is that, if the "logocentric" tradition is really characterized by the privileging of intention (or spirit [*pneuma*]) over the physical formal marking (or body [*sarx*]), then such a tradition would have nothing to fear from supplementing a merely physical text. Fish's argument overlooks the way that the "word," which Milton is initially so fearful of supplementing and later so eager to supplement, is exclusively the written word. The difficulty in Milton's position is that in his refusal to violate the inner word of conscience, he loses the ability to distinguish between conscience and the rationalist ego. Although Fish is careful to point out where Milton would not agree with his own reading of the tract (58), the very observation of such differences obscures the way in which Fish actually employs similar assumptions in his own reading. On the one hand, Fish's argument depends upon a conflation of the internal (spiritual) and external (written) word, by equating a belief in objective metaphysical truth with

60

dependence upon the weakness of a mutable written text. On the other hand, Fish (also like Milton) elides any distinction between the operations of the rationalist ego and the internal word of conscience.

We can begin to see the importance of the way that Fish employs these Miltonic assumptions, if we look at how his argument re-introduces consideration of Augustine's rule of charity. Here, Fish can make the explicit point that the rule of charity, no less than any other attempt to locate meaning in intention leads to anti-formalism. From his discussion of Milton's divorce tract, Fish concludes that the rule of charity is "really a version of the argument from intention" which "tells us that God would not require more of his creatures than they are able to perform, and therefore he would not require that they remain joined to unsuitable partners" ("Wanting" 62). Against those who would insist that the rule of charity can operate as an objective principle, Fish points out how easy it would be to disagree with Milton's interpretation by taking issue specifically with his definition of charity:

> But the rule [of charity] fails as a constraint on interpretation in the same way that intention fails; for the question of what charity means is, like the question of God's intention, an interpretive one. There is nothing to prevent Milton's opponents from defining charity differently—so that, for example, it would be charitable of God to enforce strict divorce laws because he would thus provoke men to more virtue than they would otherwise achieve—or from declaring that the "rule of charity" should not be extended to the issue of divorce. . . . In short, the "all interpreting rule" of charity must itself be interpreted in order to be applied, and if it is interpreted once, then it can always be interpreted again. (62)

According to Fish, the very possibility of disagreement in defining "charity" means that it cannot operate as an objective principle. It is important to remember that Fish is not saying that we cannot define charity or know "truth," but that all attempts to define charity or know the truth will always require that we employ definitional criteria or cognitional operations which are contextually constrained, and can, therefore, never be metaphysically or universally true (43). Notwithstanding such a conclusion, Fish would still insist that we can and must define charity. However, his point here is that the defining will never stop, because some terms (not always the same ones) will always be open for debate.

If we keep in mind that Fish's argument depends upon his own interpretation of the rule of charity, we can begin to ask whether his own anti-formalism is any less dependent upon rationalist assumptions than Milton's alleged anti-formalism. We must first, however, note the different levels of engagement on which such an inquiry can operate. In one sense, Fish's argument is implacable, because any attempt to argue that the rule of charity is not simply "a matter of interpretation," only serves as evidence against itself in the very act of arguing. Fish would point out (in a manner suspiciously similar to Milton's antiprelatical tract) that in arguing for the perspicuity of the meaning of "charity" we only serve to support his broader point that the "perspicuity" is never as clear as it might first seem, and is always settled by debate. Fish's own argument is not for a specific version of the rule of charity, but that any version of the rule of charity will always be vulnerable to further revision (interpretation). The problem is that as a meta-hermeneutic claim, such a position, according to Fish, cannot have consequences for any specific (contextually constrained) act of interpretation. Even in making such an assertion, however, his argument participates in the foundationalist assumption that knowledge can be had independent of moral considerations. In order to be consistent with Fish's own anti-foundationalism we must ask what valuative assumptions are operating in his interpretation of the rule of charity. In effect, what definition of charity (or virtue) does Fish tacitly adopt, in his attempt to make a meta-hermeneutic argument concerning the rule of charity? More importantly, what does the attendant claim, that precisely such a meta-hermeneutic position is inconsequential or inapplicable, imply about the way he allows those same valuative assumptions to operate? This approach avoids supplementing Fish's position, by not starting with an argument for the perspicuity of a specific definition of charity, and allows us to begin, instead, with an attempt to understand his interpretation within its own terms of reference. This approach also avoids making claims regarding any kind of "inaccessible assumptions," because such assumptions could admittedly never be the object of anyone's communicable thoughts. Our attention will focus instead upon the mutually perspicuous (virtually banal) observations of the valuative assumptions which enable his reading of Augustine.

Throughout the development of his position, Fish does not alter significantly his reading of *On Christian Doctrine*, which he initially presents in *Self-Consuming Artifacts*. Later renderings of Augustine's view are basically distillations of this earlier reading. One main point that Fish consistently makes (or implies) about the rule of charity is its ability to function as a "totalizing system." The unrelenting capacity of the Augustinian system to derive the same meaning out of every passage only serves to demonstrate its power:

In other words, this rule would seem to urge us to disregard context, to bypass the conventional meanings of words, and in general, to violate the integrity of language and discursive forms of thought. To such an accusation Augustine would no doubt reply, "That is exactly the point," for his assumption is that if a word or a sentence does not lead to the reign of charity, the fault lies in the eye that so misinterprets it. (*SCA* 22)

If we look more closely at Augustine's *On Christian Doctrine,* we can see that Fish's characterization of the rule of charity is misleading in two important ways: first, in spite of his apologetic rhetoric elsewhere, Fish consistently implies that the rule (like all interpretation) is predicated upon "wilful" (biased but unmotivated) manipulation of a text (only later will he conclude that the text, as such, does not exist to be manipulated); second, Fish presents the rule of allegorical interpretation in such a way that he ignores Augustine's pivotal emphasis upon the "plain sense" of Scripture.

Before making the above statement in *Self-Consuming Artifacts,* Fish presents two important quotations to demonstrate the totalizing nature of Augustine's position. In both cases, an understanding of the how these statements function within Augustine's larger argument will show how Fish's interpretation allows him later to disregard the Augustinian account:

Whatever appears in the divine Word that does not literally pertain to virtuous behavior or to truth of faith you must take to be figurative. (*OCD* 3.10.14)

Therefore in the consideration of figurative expressions a rule such as this will serve, that what is read should be subjected to diligent scrutiny until an interpretation contributing to the reign of charity is produced. (*OCD* 3.15.23)

Because of the way that Fish frames these quotations with comments about being "wholly subversive" (*SCA* 21) and "violat[ing] the integrity of language" (22), it is particularly necessary to him that he does not quote from the beginning of the next paragraph that follows the first quotation:

But since humanity is inclined to estimate sins, not on the basis of the importance of the passion involved in them, but rather on the basis of their own customs, so that they consider a man culpable in accordance with the way men are reprimanded and condemned ordinarily in their own place and time, and, at the same time consider them to be virtuous and praiseworthy in so far as the customs of those among whom they live would so incline them, it so happens that if Scripture commends something despised by the customs of the listeners, or condemns what those customs do not condemn, they take the Scriptural locution as figurative if they accept it as an authority. (*OCD* 3.10.15)

Here Augustine is describing the kind of reading that the rule of charity is designed to remedy, in that it provides an objective standard by which to judge cultural assumptions. Because some cultural assumptions may be conducive to the love of God and neighbor, while others may not, the rule of charity allows us to determine when to interpret a passage figuratively or not, rather than depend upon those cultural biases. Although Fish never explicitly "misrepresents" Augustine's view, he consistently implies that the rule of charity is somehow only a justification for cultural biases. (Only later in his career will Fish cite the rule as an example of that first critical step down the anti-formalist road.) The rhetorical effect of Fish's presentation of the rule of charity is to reverse Augustine's insistence that the rule of charity can operate as an objective constraint on cultural biases. Fish might insist that he does not impute any subjectivism to Augustine's position; however, he does something much more subtle than that. In *Is There a Text?* Fish uses Augustine's theory as an example of the express function of an interpretive community. This shift is pivotal, because it allows Fish to talk about the rule of charity specifically as a cultural phenomenon (within a community), rather than as a claim which stands in opposition to cultural biases. This shift, however, simply makes explicit the way that Fish has been implicitly treating Augustine's position all along. Once again, only in later writings will Fish make the argument that the question of how to define charity will always be open for debate, and thereby leads to anti-formalism. However, his very ability to make such an argument has been implicit from the beginning, because of the way that he neglects Augustine's insistence upon the "plain sense" of Scripture.

Although we find his most lengthy treatment of the *De Doctrina* in *Self-Consuming Artifacts*, Fish provides his most balanced presentation of the rule of charity in *Is There a Text?*

> If only you should come upon something that does not seem at first to bear this meaning, that "does not literally pertain to virtuous behavior or to the truth of faith," you are then to take it "to be figurative" and proceed to scrutinize it "until an interpretation contributing to the reign of charity is produced." (*ITTC* 170)

We can designate this representation of Augustine's position as "more balanced," because of Fish's judicious use of the qualifying phrase, "if only." The more basic problem still remains, however, in that Fish never mentions Augustine's explicit insistence that the rule of charity itself depends upon a previously understood "plain sense" of Scripture. Augustine assumes that a clear understanding of "virtuous behavior" and the "truth of faith" can be learned only from the "literal sense" of

Scripture, and that such a reading is required in order to discern not only the rule of charity as an interpretive principle, but charity itself. Basically, Fish ignores book 1 of Augustine's treatise, in spite of the fact that Augustine would have insisted that book 1 is the only part that deals with the most basic and necessary "knowledge of God":

> Thus the Holy Spirit has magnificently and wholesomely modulated the Holy Scriptures so that the more open places present themselves to hunger and the more obscure places may deter a disdainful attitude. *Hardly anything may be found in these obscure places which is not found plainly said elsewhere.*
> (*OCD* 2.6.8; emphasis added)

> Among those things which are said openly in Scripture are to be found all those things which involve faith, the mores of living, and that hope and charity which we have discussed in the previous book [i.e., bk.1]. (*OCD* 2.9.14)

By completely omitting consideration of passages like these, Fish's interpretation is at least misleading, in that it makes allegorical reading the central feature of Augustine's teaching, rather than openly pointing out that the allegorical method is actually the most superfluous part. Within his own discussion of Augustine's *On Christian Doctrine*, Fish cites an essay by Joseph Mazzeo (*SCA* 23). Because Mazzeo makes a point very similar to the one being made here, it is revealing that Fish could have presented Augustine's allegorical theory in a more balanced way:

> The first and most important thing to say about St. Augustine's conception of allegory and his techniques of biblical exegesis is that he considered them, in the last analysis, relatively unimportant. All of the teaching on faith and morals necessary to salvation is quite plain in Scripture. (Mazzeo 5)

Initially, Fish needs to obscure Augustine's insistence upon the primacy of "those things which are said openly," in order to support his characterization of Augustinian hermeneutics as a "totalizing system."[5] Later on, however, when he appropriates the stance of faith in articulating his own position, it becomes even more critical that Augustine's notion of "faith" be separated from the illusory "common sense" of objectivist epistemology. Still later, by the time he reverses his alignment of dialectic to support rhetoric, he can then dismiss the rule of charity, by pointing out that it is based on an illusory notion of objective truth.

This series of developments also reminds us how such talk about charity, as an "objective principle" taken from the "plain sense" of Scripture, sounds much like the legal discourse that Fish is so busy debunking in *Doing What Comes Naturally*. Fish would insist that

Augustine is simply mistaken in thinking that charity can be known objectively. The difference, however, lies not so much in their competing views of charity, but in their different conceptions of mind-independent reality. Because Fish takes his characterization of objective truth from the Miltonic idioms of early-modern rationalism, he must consistently render Augustine's belief as contradictory, just as he does Milton's.

We can begin to see the central differences between Augustine and Milton, if we compare Milton's anxiety about the scriptural text with Augustine's apparent lack of concern about similar issues. Although Augustine began writing *On Christian Doctrine* around 396 A.D., he did not write book 4 until over thirty years later (Robertson ix). One of the important differences that appears between the writing of book 2 and book 4 is that by 427 Augustine had substantially revised his thinking regarding those translations of Scripture which are most authoritative. Initially he indicates that the *Itala* translation is one of the better ones, and specifically cites the Greek Septuagint as a superior source text (rather than Hebrew ones) for emending Latin translations (*OCD* 2.15.22). However, by the time Augustine writes book 4, he claims that he "shall not follow the Septuagint translators," choosing instead to name Jerome's translation as best (4.7.15). There were obviously several factors which influenced the change within Augustine's thinking over the course of thirty years. In one sense, such a change in position might hardly be worth noting, except that it highlights the nature of the difference between Augustine's and Milton's understanding of Scripture. Earlier we observed how Milton's objectivist epistemology led him to reject altogether the frailty of a written textual object in favor of the internal word of conscience. Augustine does not have the same difficulty in managing the textual inconsistencies between various translations and manuscripts and in negotiating the accompanying ecclesiastical debates. The reason for this is that Augustine never views Scripture primarily as a book. His understanding of scriptural authority is inextricable from his understanding of the Church as a believing community. According to Augustine, because our knowledge of correct inference can never ensure that our propositions (either as premises or conclusions) are true (*OCD* 2.34.52), human reason cannot finally be trusted as a guide to knowledge. At the same time, because of the necessary role that belief plays in knowledge, the choice is never between faith and reason, but between competing beliefs (*Confessions* 6.5). According to Augustine, then, the question is which set of beliefs will lead to knowledge. More specifically, the question is whom to trust, because Augustine does not view differing faiths as primarily abstract systems, but as believing communites.

In this respect, there is great significance in the fact that Augustine does not describe his development in the *Confessions* as simply a change from one belief system to another, but as a movement from one community to another, often connected to specific encounters with specific people. However, rather than privilege the authority of the Church over Scripture, thereby removing the ability of Scripture to guard against cultural biases, Augustine holds the two in dynamic tension. In effect, the "Word of God" is simultaneously and necessarily constituted by both the believing community and the message which is independent of that community, together resulting in a continuous incarnation of eternal truth within time. In witnessing the congruity between the message and the believing community, Augustine was compelled to believe the message. This is why his faith did not come unraveled in shifting his view of the authoritative text from the Septuagint to a translation based on the Hebrew.

Because Milton begins with an understanding of Scripture primarily as a textual reality, he cannot avoid eventually abandoning the corruptible written text altogether, in favor of a completely subjective (and individual) "Word of God." Because Augustine does not begin with the primacy of the isolated individual mastering a reified text, he is never forced to separate the authority of Scripture from the authority of the believing community, in the way that Milton does from the outset.[6] Milton's ability to move from the mere possibility of textual corruption to a radical anti-formalism is predicated upon a deep suspicion toward the historical community through which he received the scriptural text:

> The external scripture, particularly the New Testament, has often been liable to corruption and is, in fact, corrupt. This has come about because it has been committed to the care of various untrustworthy authorities, has been collected together from an assortment of manuscripts, and has survived in a medley of transcripts. (*CD* 587-88)

Augustine is not overly concerned about the residual effects of textual corruption, because he believes that the power of the message is sufficient to maintain the integrity of its guardians, while Milton uses the same issue of textual corruption to argue for a radically individual dependence upon the Spirit (587-90). Augustine is finally able to maintain the mind-independent status of scriptural truth, because he does not locate that truth exclusively in a text, and therefore never participates in the foundationalist assumptions which later make solipsism inevitable for the rationalist ego. Many people today (as post-romantic moderns) might see Augustine's view of submission to authority as a tragic flaw in an otherwise great philosophic mind. The problem with such a perception is that, while it presumes the truth of modern objectivist epistemology, it obscures the potential in Augustine's thinking to provide an alternative to the aporias of foundationalist self-destruction.

In order to begin discussing more directly Augustine's view of rationalism, we must briefly address the issue of his relation to Platonism. The issue is complicated by both the vast range of philosophic projects which have used the name "Platonic," for one reason or another, and the almost equally wide range of interpretations of "Augustinian" texts. Moreover, these complications are multiplied exponentially by the ongoing possibility of questioning the differences between the various "Platonisms" and Augustine's representation (or misrepresentation) of a given Platonic teaching. We shall avoid the majority of these complexities by focusing upon a couple of very simple assertions regarding Platonism, which will help us to clarify Augustine's view of rationalism in general. There is an obvious sense in which Augustine could be labeled as a "Platonic" thinker, because of the many ways in which he incorporates Platonic ideas and images into his writing (cf. Copleston 73-74). However, if we understand "Platonism" as that kind of formalism which equates rational order with the supreme good (e.g., *Republic* 540a-b; *Gorgias* 506e), rather than using it as a name for all types of metaphysical realism, then Augustine is clearly not a Platonist. Such a qualification is also justified in view of Augustine's own explicit attempts to reject what he perceived Platonism to be.

If we look briefly at Augustine's *Confessions*, we can see the character of that rejection. Many of the passages in the *Confessions* where Augustine expresses fascination with his own cognitive process function as part of a larger argument, which might be described as a psychological version of the "argument from design" for the existence of God. In each case, whether it be a description of childhood language acquisition (1.8), or adult sense perception (7.17), or his experience of memory (10.16-18), his observations consistently depend upon an ability to think outside the rationalist categories of subject and object. It can be very difficult for readers today to appreciate this element within Augustine's thinking, without first becoming genuinely confused by what seems to be a continual shifting of categories. For example, in book 12, as he wrestles with the possible meanings of the phrase "formless matter" in Genesis 1:2, he seems to be doing little more than trying to make sense of the passage as a rationalist might, making deductions from his logical first principles (12.3-11). Yet his simultaneous appeal to the "voice" within (12.15) and God's "whisper" (12.16), in helping him understand those same verses, seems to indicate some kind of radical subjectivism. Such perceptions, however, depend upon the deployment of rationalist categories which Augustine would find incoherent. The psychological arguments from design also show us that Augustine makes no distinction between his own mind and the created order. Because his own perceptions and cognitive actions are as much a part of "nature" as anything else, and as much a gift of grace, he makes no arbitrary distinctions between the various aspects of his trusting attempts to know truth.

Because he begins with the creaturely condition of his own being in relationship, rather than as a rationalist ego mastering nature, he explicitly rejects Platonism because of its tendency towards pride:

> For I had now begun to wish to be thought wise. I was full of self-esteem, which was a punishment of my own making. I thought to have deplored my state, but instead my *knowledge only bred self-conceit*. For was I not without charity, which builds on the firm foundation of humility, that is, on Jesus Christ? But how could I expect that Platonist books would ever teach me charity? (*Confessions* 7.20)

He goes on to point out that the difference between Platonism and Christianity is the "difference between presumption and confession, between those who see the goal that they must reach, but cannot see the road by which they are to reach it, and those who see the road to that blessed country which is meant to be no mere vision but our home" (7.20). Augustine makes this same point in his *Homilies on the Gospel of St. John*, where he emphasizes that the difference between Christian faith (epitomized in Christ's life of charity) and "philosophy" (epitomized by the prideful self-deception of reason) is the difference between pilgrimage and speculation:

> [Philosophers] were able to see that which is, but they saw it from afar: they were unwilling to hold the lowliness of Christ, in which ship they might have arrived in safety at that which they were able to see from afar; and the cross of Christ appeared vile to them. The sea has to be crossed, and dost thou despise the wood? . . . There is no means of passing to the fatherland unless borne by the wood. (*Homilies* 2.4)

Whether Augustine is accurate in his characterization of Platonism or not, what he is rejecting is the attempt to separate knowledge from ethical considerations. His view is similar to that of Fish, in that he indicts the pride of rationalist formalism, but the ethical grounds upon which he does so are radically different. Whereas Fish tends to locate ethical

69

considerations exclusively in the predetermining assumptions (beliefs) which shape our interpretations and actions, Augustine emphasizes both the recognition of beliefs which shape our knowledge, as well as the need for ethical action (life of charity) in following the example of Christ as a consequence of faith.

The other important difference between Augustine's argument for humility and Fish's is that although Augustine rejects rationalist objectivism, his view still implies the existence of a mind-independent reality. Although this truth is mind-independent (and even metaphysical) it can only be manifest and communicated through human relations:

> Deinde ipsa caritas, quae sibi homines inuicem nodo unitatis adstringit, non haberet aditum refundendorum et quasi miscendorum sibimet animorum, si homines per homines nihil discerent. (*DDC*, SAA Prœmium 6)

> For charity itself, which draws humans together in a bond of unity, would not have a means of infusing souls and almost mixing them together if humans could teach nothing to humans.
> (*OCD* Prologue 6; adaptation of Robertson trans.)

Augustine points out how this belief in a personal yet transcendent truth provides a basis for humility, by quoting 1 Corinthians 4:7: "For what have we which we have not received? And if we have received it why do we glory as if we had not received it?" (Prol. 8). Because all knowledge is necessarily of God who is the truth (Prol. 8), there is no basis for pride, as though somehow the truth belonged to a human individual. Fish effectively makes this same point in his discussion of the tension between "pride and despair," that preachers face within Augustine's account (*SCA* 40). Here again we see part of the rhetorical effectiveness in Fish's later re-alignment of the categories of rhetoric and philosophy, when he identifies objectivism rather than rhetoric with the complacent status quo (*DWCN* 474). This is why Fish can incorporate the valorization of humility within his own rejection of objective truth, as he maintains his use of the dialectical (self-consuming) form while rejecting the objective truth upon which it depends.

Augustine's position helps to show why Fish's attempt to employ this kind of "rhetorical humility" finally fails. The basis for humility in Augustine's view is the recognition of gift: "what have we which we have not received?" Earlier we noted that within Fish's view "true humility" is not possible. Augustine might point out that the reason for this is that a true "gift" is not possible within Fish's system. This also explains why Fish is skeptical about *caritas,* in that his terms of reference cannot

70

avoid rendering "gift-love" (or self-sacrifice) as incoherent. The perception of "gift" must always be an illusion, within Fish's argument, because our notions of "other" can only be a function of those inaccessible assumptions which presently constitute the self. Fish could, however, respond to such an objection by arguing that his view does not make gift-giving impossible, but instead recognizes that all gifts can only function as such within a culturally constrained set of values about what is appropriate as a gift, and within social practices concerning what constitutes a recognizable act of giving or receiving, and so forth. In this sense, Fish's argument for the "less-hypocritical false humility" of anti-foundationalism directly parallels Augustine's argument for humility, in that it is based on a similar recognition that the "truth" we perceive, however dimly, is not really our own, but is generated by the assumptions we share to varying degrees with those around us. The curious difference is that the "immutable God," "who is truth" in Augustine's system, is replaced in Fish's by the interpretive gods of agnosis who are ever present yet inaccessible. There is a striking parallel between Fish's inaccessible yet inescapable assumptions and Augustine's view, that God is "most hidden from us and yet the most present amongst us" (*Confessions* 1.4). The primary difference between these two hidden realities is that Augustine's God is personal and, as such, has chosen self-disclosure. One other important difference is that, even in these initial comments from the *De Doctrina,* we can already see Augustine's use of the multiple senses in which God is both *veritas* and *caritas,* leading us into book 1, where his central concern is precisely the identification of both these realities with the Triune God. While there is a sense in which Fish's pantheon of interpretive assumptions can be genuinely identified with the sources of "truth" and "charity," their unrelenting concealment is a function of the incapacity of subpersonal realities for self-disclosure. Again, this is consistent with the way in which Fish's argument renders incoherent the concept of volition in general. However, even if Fish were to insist that human "choice" does operate, in some very qualified sense, because these interpretive assumptions consitute the grounding for the possibility of such quasi-volitional activity, there is no sense in which these mute gods of agnosis could ever choose self-disclosure.

Ultimately, Fish's rejection of the rule of charity is based on his foreclosure against the possibility of knowledge of God, because he always defines such knowledge in either rationalist or subjectivist terms. As long as claims about the knowledge of God are open to interpretation and debate, the rule of charity is equally open to interpretation. This is also consistent with Fish's repeated treatment of Milton's prose. In his examination of both Milton's divorce tract and *Christian Doctrine,* Fish observes that Milton is taken "down the anti-formalist road" by making the rule of charity into "God's intention" ("Wanting" 57-58; *NSFS* 292; *DWCN* 8-9). Milton argues that certain actions are wrong (uncharitable) because they are not in accord with God's character ("Wanting" 57-58; *DWCN* 8-9). Because Fish never mentions the objectivist nature of Milton's ideas about the "knowledge of God" (discussed above), he is able to treat Milton's idea of "God's intention" as though it implied a subjectivist position—acknowledging all the while that, of course, Milton would object to such a reading of his prose. The deeper problem that emerges out of this misrepresentation is the way that Fish's position, in spite of its claims to be consistently anti-foundationalist, still supports the modern objectivist bifurcation of knowledge and affection. Fish might respond that he makes no such division because he already holds that "knowledge" in the objectivist sense does not exist, and that really desire (corporate or individual) is all that knowledge claims can ever be. However, as we shall see, Fish's argument avoids considering the affective dimension of human knowing only by ingesting the idea of motivation.

Initially, Fish seems to make the common poststructuralist "observation" (itself motivated) that all knowledge claims are motivated. By making his own claim into a non-statement, Fish simultaneously accounts for motivation or bias while also banning it from all further discussion. What drops out of his account is the Augustinian view that knowledge is directly connected to inter-personal affection. Augustine's position is importantly different from the Platonic view which regards the human consciousness as constituted by desires in such a way that the desire for rational knowledge is the supreme part of the soul. Augustine points out that purely rational knowledge is impersonal and cannot, therefore, be a sufficient end in itself. Like Fish, Augustine admits that his knowledge claims are biased; unlike Fish, however, he states openly that he is motivated by the desire to know God in relationship, rather than by the desire for mastery over objects.[7] Moreover, Augustine argues that all pursuit of knowledge which does not have its ultimate root in the creaturely desire for creator will lead to the debasement of humans. Fish's argument reverts to the rationalist fact-value distinction, because of the paralysis it creates, by banning the issue of motivation from consideration (making "bias" a non-issue). By his own terms, the admission that "everything is motivated" (or contextually constrained) is the same as saying that "nothing is motivated." However, because, according to Fish, we cannot avoid holding our own views as though they are anything other than universally true, and at the same time our most basic assumptions are mutually inaccessible, we must simply make truth claims without being able to make any allowance for our own biases or those of others—critical self-awareness is an illusion.

Obviously, Fish could insist that his position does not necessitate such conclusions, as demonstrated by the very existence of many of his political arguments in *There's No Such Thing as Free Speech*. Whether or not his politics are justified by his position or non-position, his argument does nothing to oppose the covert knowledge/power imperative of technocratic objectivist epistemology. Fish would insist that his position is different from that of the objectivist, in that he admits that his claims to knowledge are motivated by his own desire for power, rather than claiming to be "objective." However, that admission is precisely the only difference, and his own argument disallows the privileging of such self-awareness. The value of such an admission could be legitimated only within an ethical context which recognizes humility. This brings us again to Fish's repeated contrast between the "proud formalist" and the "humble anti-formalist." But such a contrast is no longer tenable even for Fish, because the oxymoronic notion of "unmotivated bias," which ensures the implacability of his position, also ensures that humility and pride cannot be distinguished.

Fish's argument, despite his insistence to the contrary, still implies a kind of latent solipsism, in that the rigorous attempt to avoid formalism never admits even the consideration of mind-independent reality. This is why his "interpretive communites" degenerate into matrices of interpretive assumptions which collectively perform as engines for their own transformation (*DWCN* 150). His argument therefore avoids solipsism, not by recognizing the existence of other subjectivities, but by conceiving of personal reality as the material experience of being spoken by interpretive assumptions which belong to no one. In effect, solipsism is avoided only by the annihilation of the *solus*. Because Fish's position also still depends upon those rationalist first principles which it collapses, his own argument falls into a supplementary dependence upon foundationalism. The attempt to argue for or against a position, on the grounds that it is biased or unbiased, is incoherent, because interpretive assumptions (or biases) are inescapable. This is why we are not concerned here to "expose," in some facile manner, the hidden biases in Fish's argument, as though the very existence of such assumptions constituted a grounds for rejecting his position. Instead, we can see that Fish's ability to employ Augustine's theory in support of his own position depends upon including Augustine within his Miltonic characterization of the logocentric tradition, and that Fish's own position is dependent upon the foundationalism it rejects. This recognition, however, results in more than simply acknowledging the postmodern banalities concerning the totalizing nature of supplementarity. When we remember that the doctrine of supplementarity is itself an anti-foundationalist belief, we realize that we have never escaped the objectivist epistemology upon which that anti-foundationalism depends (as a self-consuming antecedent). Anti-foundationalism does not refute the possibility of mind-independent truth, as much as it demonstrates that rationalism is self-contradictory.

This raises a new set of questions about ouselves as readers. Are we, as contemporary readers of Fish or Augustine, capable of reading or thinking without tacitly employing the foundationalist/anti-foundationalist dichotomy in our most basic assumptions? The next chapter attempts to answer this question by looking more closely at how Fish describes this totalizing opposition in his discussion of "rhetoric." The attempt to answer this question will also involve other questions that have developed out of our reading thus far. Is it only a coincidence that one of the primary arguments in Milton's *Christian Doctrine* is against the Trinity (which subsists in a relation of charity), and that Fish effectively learns from reading Milton that the rule of charity really means nothing? Can we know charity (contextually or otherwise)? Even given Augustine's view that the pivotal epistemic question is whom to trust, we are still left with the question of how to decide whom to trust.

CHAPTER FOUR

Rhetoric

One important aspect of Fish's writing, which has often been obscured by the analysis thus far, is a certain rhetorical appeal that can best be described by its effects. His arguments maintain a persistent but intangible sense of "reasonableness" that tends to disarm anyone trying to analyze them; whenever an objection is raised against his position, there often remains a nagging doubt that somehow Fish would insist that he never implied anything so ridiculous as that which the alleged objection ascribes to him. The problem is also complicated by the nature of his argument regarding the way in which shared interpretive assumptions constitute mutual understanding. Given such a condition, is it possible to offer a genuine alternative to his position which is not either a function of those same assumptions or else incoherent? Nor is it sufficient that we should try to avoid "misrepresenting" Fish's arguments by inadvertently doing to them what Milton does to Matthew 7:19 (i.e., reversing the "perspicuous" meaning by recontextualizing the verse) ("Wanting" 54-56). The temptation is genuine, in that it would now be relatively easy to "recontextualize" Fish's arguments so that their "perspicuous" meaning could reveal the Augustinian position that Fish has been unwittingly/wittingly holding all along. However, the situation is still more convoluted, because according to Fish's broader position, all that anyone ever does in the act of interpretation is what Milton does to Matthew 7:19 (once again we meet the issue of "unmotivated bias"). Beyond Fish's argument for the perspicuity of the primacy of interpretive assumptions remains the question of whether his own argument has been able to extricate itself from the very metaphysics it would declare inconsequential. Is it possible to make rhetoric perform for social relations those operations previously reserved for metaphysical discourse, without ascribing an ontological status to rhetoric itself? The attempt to answer this question leads us to consider Fish's account of the relation between rhetoric and philosophy.

In the interview appended to *There's No Such Thing as Free Speech*, where Fish mentions the shaping influences of Milton and Augustine on his thinking about "faith" (292-93), he also makes a connection between his belief in the "primacy of rhetoric" and the teachings of the ancient sophists (290-91). He then discusses the rhetorical benefits of describing himself as a "contemporary sophist" (291). The link with the ancient sophists allows Fish to talk about "rhetoric" as a marginalized tradition of anti-essentialism (or anti-foundationalism), but it also allows him to link that "tradition" with his own argument for the operation of those inescapable and inaccessible "interpretive constraints" (assumptions). Fish's comments within the interview are based on his more detailed argument in *Doing What Comes Naturally*, where he attempts to draw a parallel between the contemporary debate between foundationalism and anti-foundationalism, and the more ancient debate between philosophy and rhetoric. Earlier we noted the general terms of Fish's comparison, as he presents it in his essay entitled "Rhetoric." We shall now examine his argument in greater detail, in order to understand the precise way in which Fish's deployment of the stance of "faith" not only attenuates his own dependence upon the principle of reason, but also conceals the need for such "faith" to have content.

The argument of Fish's essay entitled "Rhetoric" is ostensibly concerned with supporting a primarily historical claim. The attempt to link present-day anti-foundationalists with the ancient sophists is part of his broader view that "the quarrel between philosophy and rhetoric, survives every sea change in the history of Western thought" (*DWCN* 478). Fish cites, among others, Protagoras and Isocrates as examples of *homo rhetoricus*, who, like the anti-essentialists today, "recognize only accidental as opposed to essential being," because they insist that the human "realm of the probable" is the only one relevant for consideration (479-83). *Homo rhetoricus* is not concerned with some inaccessible "abstract truth, but with the truth that emerges in the context of distinctly human conversations," because a "God's-eye view" is both unavailable and irrelevant (485-86). "Truth" is then defined as that which is humanly understood within the present conversation, because it is simply all that we ever have. Fish goes on to suggest that the debate between *homo seriosus* (the essentialists) and *homo rhetoricus* is incommensurable because it can only be answered from within the assumptions of one side or the other (483-84). We have already mentioned briefly (in chap. 2) the general problems involved in Fish's claim for the existence of such a totalizing dichotomy, but we shall now attend to the specific terms upon which the dichotomy depends.[1]

Before proceeding any further, though, we can already note a couple of elements in his argument which indicate that the dichotomy is not as stable as Fish suggests. First, when Isocrates the rhetorician argued for the primacy of "speech," he used the Greek word *logos*; his belief in the power of rhetoric (persuasion) was based on a more basic belief in the objective power of "the word" (Harris and Taylor xi). Second, Fish's description of *homo rhetoricus* sounds surprisingly similar to classic descriptions of the "philosophic" (wisdom-loving) life epitomized by Socrates. In fact, Fish's characterization of "the sophist" directly parallels Leo Strauss's depiction of the philosophic life as a quest for wisdom that cannot be complete without ceasing to be itself. As such an undertaking, philosophy can never become wisdom itself, with the implication that "all solutions are questionable":

> The right way of life cannot be fully established except by an understanding of the nature of man and the nature of man cannot be fully clarified except by an understanding of the nature of the whole. Therefore, the right way of life cannot be established metaphysically except by a completed metaphysics, and therefore the right way of life remains questionable. (Strauss 297-98)

The introduction of such a comparison may seem surprising, in view of the way that Strauss and Fish might typically be contrasted as the extreme opposite ends of an epistemic continuum. But if the philosophic life is based on the "questionable" (debatable) nature of human knowledge claims, it proves to be very similar to Fish's version of the rhetorical life. These two initial observations raise questions about the "historical" basis for Fish's characterization of the dichotomy between philosophy and rhetoric.

Before we examine Fish's historical claims, we must first delineate the different senses that Fish attaches to the term "rhetoric," which allow his argument to function in the way that it does. The manner in which Fish presents the opposition between philosophy and rhetoric is important, because it bears directly on his broader rejection of the possibility of transcendence. He begins his account with the explication of a speech by the demon Belial in Milton's *Paradise Lost* (*DWCN* 471-74). Fish points out that Belial's speech is a classic depiction of the dangers of rhetoric, as defined by its opponents the "philosophers" (objectivists):

> I have lingered so long over this passage because we can extrapolate from it almost all of the binary oppositions in relation to which rhetoric has received its (largely negative) definition: inner/outer, deep/surface, essential/peripheral, unmediated/mediated, clear/colored, necessary/contingent, straightforward/angled, abiding/fleeting, reason/passion, things/words, realities/illusions, fact/opinion, neutral/partisan. (474)

These binaries are all in keeping with the characterization of rhetoric as "eloquence," or "fine language" (475). However, Fish goes on to distil from these binaries "three basic oppositions" which characterize the rhetoric-philosophy debate, and in doing so, he ascribes to rhetoric a much more substantial status than simply "fine language":

> First, between a truth that exists independently of all perspectives and points of view and the many truths that emerge and seem perspicuous when a particular perspective or point of view has been established and is in force; second, an opposition between true knowledge, which is knowledge as it exists apart from any and all systems of belief, and the knowledge, which because it flows from some or other system of belief, is incomplete and partial (in the sense of biased); and third, an opposition between a self or consciousness that is turned outward in an effort to apprehend and attach itself to truth and true knowledge and a self or consciousness that is turned inward in the direction of its own prejudices, which, far from being transcended, continue to inform its every word and action. (474)

Two immediate points are here worth noting: although this characterization of the debate is allegedly from the side of the "philosophers" (478), the opposition has already been made into an unavoidable dichotomy and is presented in a manner that already participates in the perspectival language dictated by such a totalizing dichotomy (all assessments are from either one perspective or the other); second, the dichotomy depends upon a characterization of the objectivist position, such that "self" is equated with "consciousness." The full significance of this second point will become apparent only in chapter 7, but here we need to examine the dichotomy more closely.

In the second part of the essay, Fish shifts his characterization of the debate between rhetoric and philosophy so that it more openly favors the rhetorical (anti-essentialist) position, by offering the counter-arguments of those sophists and contemporary anti-essentialists who oppose the belief in transcendent truth. Fish's use of the term "rhetoric" now expands from simply "eloquence" to include "persuasion" in general, but, more importantly, a belief in the primacy of persuasion, such that "knowledge" can only ever mean "being convinced" (479-81). The implications of this significant shift become evident only when we realize that Fish can now equate "rhetoric" with "argument" as both "the act of arguing," and as a belief in "the primacy of argument" (persuasion) in all human communication (497-98). Hereafter, any attempt to argue against the rhetorical position can always be turned against itself in the very act of "arguing" (being rhetorical). This is the same strategy that Fish uses to show that *caritas* cannot provide a constraint on interpreta-

78

tion ("Wanting" 62), and this is the reason Fish has proposed for Milton's strategy of immobility in his antiprelatical tract (43-46). The totalizing character of Fish's argument for rhetoric appears in his reassertion that the argument between "rhetoric" (anti-essentialism) and "philosophy" (rationalism/logic) has always been part of human existence:

> But it would seem, from the evidence marshalled in this essay, that something is always happening to the way we think, and that it is always the same something, a tug-of-war between two views of human life and its possibilities, no one of which can ever gain complete and lasting ascendancy because in the very moment of its triumphant articulation each turns back in the direction of the other. (*DWCN* 501)

The assertion is really no different from that stated in part one of the essay, where he first offers the totalizing dichotomy, except that now "argument" itself has been equated with "rhetoric." As a result, in a parry of supreme sophistic brilliance, Fish reduces everything to rhetoric (argument) in the very act of declaring parity between the rhetorical and philosophical positions. Because rhetoric *is* argumentation, the realm of possible disagreements between rhetoric and philosophy will always be constituted by argumentative considerations (rhetoric itself). The problem is that (once again), although Fish finally rejects the distinction between the two categories by concluding that everything is rhetorical, his rejection continues to depend upon the initial dichotomy. What if reason is never claimed as something independent of rhetoric in the first place?

At this point it is helpful to compare Fish's historical claims concerning rhetoric with Walter Ong's account of the relation between rhetoric and logic. There are several respects in which Ong's argument actually supports and helps to clarify Fish's historical claim. Yet there is another sense in which Ong's position makes impossible the broader argument that Fish attempts. Ong's view of the relation between rhetoric and logic developed out of his study of the character and influence of the teachings of Peter Ramus. Previous to Ramus, the study of "Rhetoric" (following Cicero) was divided into five parts: *inventio* ("discovery of 'arguments'"), *dispositio* (arrangement of arguments—sometimes called *iudicium*), *elocutio* (adorning the arguments with eloquent words—style), *memoria* (memorizing the entire speech for presentation), *pronuntiatio* (delivery technique) (Ong, Introduction 156). At the same time, logic (or dialectic) was generally understood to consist of two parts: *inventio* and *judicium* (156). The overlap between these two parts of logic and the first two parts of rhetoric is significant, in that, notwithstanding medieval attempts to make logic a theoretically independent "science" (Ong, *Ramus* 59-63), logic was not primarily used as something independent of rhetorical disputation (Ong, *Rhetoric* 5-6). Thus the terms "dialectic" and "logic" were generally used interchangeably to indicate oral debate (5). The equation between "dialectic" and "logic" persists after Ramus (as evidenced by Milton's title, *Artis Logicae*), but the basis for that synonymy is reversed: it results from the complete removal of the element of speech from the term "dialectic," rather than from any persisting sense of orality within the term "logic" (Ong, *Ramus* 9). What was unique in Ramist educational reforms was not the confusion of rhetoric with logic (they had always been mixed), but the attempt to make them totally distinct (Ong, Introduction 158). Ramus simply reduced rhetoric to *elocutio* (style) and *pronuntiatio* (delivery) while making *inventio* and *judicium* the exclusive domains of dialectic (logic) (157). *Memoria* was effectively removed from consideration as an art, because Ramist method (dialectic) itself was "an elaborate structure designed to implement recall," and because the advent of printing had diminished the "need for exhaustively cultivated memory" (157). These two developments—the attempt to separate rhetoric from logic completely and the removal of memory from the generally assumed account of discursive practice—will have direct implications for our consideration of Fish's arguments. We should already note, however, that Ramus was not at all justified in making the arbitrary separation between rhetoric and logic:

> Ramus's distinction between the two arts, however admirable its aim, was insecure not only because it laid rhetoric open to the charge of meretriciousness but, more profoundly, because it was based on ukase prompted by impatience and pedagogical convenience rather than on any profound insight into the nature of thought and expression. (159)

At the most basic level, Ramus distorted logic by ignoring the way that it "grew out of reflection on the methodology of discussion and dispute" (159), but he also distorted rhetoric by denying the central role that reason plays in persuasion.

The development of Ramist dialectic involved more than the arbitrary separation of rhetoric from logic; it was also part of broader epistemological developments that would culminate in the work of early-modern rationalists like Descartes:

> Ramist dialectic represented a drive toward thinking not only of the universe but of thought itself in terms of the spatial models apprehended by

sight. In this context the notion of knowledge as word and the personalist orientation of cognition and of the universe which this notion implies is due to atrophy. Dialogue itself will drop more than ever out of dialectic. Persons, who alone speak (and in whom alone knowledge and science exist), will be eclipsed insofar as the world is thought of as an assemblage of the sort of things which vision apprehends—objects or surfaces. (Ong, *Ramus* 9)

This is not to claim that Ramism is solely responsible for the predominance of ocular metaphors that have shaped Western epistemology since before Plato. Ramism is rather an intensification of that tendency to an unprecedented degree, an intensification enabled by the culmination of certain tendencies in medieval logic (e.g., Peter of Spain) (55-75) and early Renaissance logic (e.g., Agricola) (125-30) and by the advent of print culture which made the chirographic character of Learned Latin even more visual in orientation through the use of bifurcating tables (8). More importantly, Ramism directly parallels some key components within Fish's argument for "rhetoric" (or anti-essentialism). On the one hand, the "spatial" modelling that Fish initially sets out to reject by developing reader-response theory (*ITTC* 167) precisely matches the characteristics of Ramist logic, and thus Fish seems to set his arguments in opposition to such thinking. However, his attempt to make a radical distinction between "rhetoric" (as only eloquence) and "philosophy" (objective logic as "pure thought" independent of speech) is similar to the arbitrary Ramist division between rhetoric and dialectic (itself a culmination of the Scholastic "quantification of thought") (Ong, *Ramus* 53-63). Of course, Fish rejects the objectivist assumptions that underlie Ramus's project, but that is precisely the difficulty. In order for Fish to support his claim that "everything is rhetorical" he must maintain that the argument (rhetorical deliberation) between philosophy and rhetoric is always ongoing. However, in order for that "argument" to be ongoing, the opposition between the two sides, and the dichotomy on which that opposition depends, cannot be collapsed. In order for Fish to support the claim that "philosophy" (objectivism) is finally subsumed within rhetoric (as argument), he must simultaneously maintain that dichotomy in order to maintain the argument (rhetoric). Therefore, Fish's ability to argue for the primacy of rhetoric depends upon his maintaining the questionable Ramist division between rhetoric and "logic."

Before we examine the last part of Fish's essay on "Rhetoric," one more point is germane regarding the intellectual and linguistic context in which Ramism developed. Although Augustine, Ramus and Milton all wrote and spoke Latin fluently, the works of Ramus and Milton participated in a "Learned Latin" culture that was qualitatively different from Augustine's (Ong, *Rhetoric* 17). The Latin of Ramus and Milton was taught specifically for the purpose of "speaking" (debating and delivering speeches) in the language of the authoritative classical texts, but the language remained only "residually oral," in that no one for centuries had been able to speak Latin who was not also able to read it (Ong, *Orality* 163-64). The chirographic basis of medieval and Renaissance Latin resulted in two developments relevant to our present considerations: first, it encouraged "an extreme deference for the written word which verged on superstition" (Ong, *Rhetoric* 17); second, in spite of a "residually oral mentality," Learned Latin was "opaque by comparison with a text in one's mother tongue," because the Latin lacked the mixture of "unconscious and conscious elements" commonly operative in a living rather than text-bound language (Ong, *Orality* 163). Without exploring here the broader consequences of this pedagogical legacy, we can at least observe that the chirographic control of Latin encouraged a visual orientation, further to ways already mentioned, which regarded words as "things seen" (external spatial objects) rather than "speech heard" (internalized temporal action) (71-72). Thus the relative opacity of Learned Latin would also encourage the belief in static or determinate meaning. Some specific implications of this linguistic context will become obvious only once we begin to compare some aspects of Milton's theology with Augustine's.

In the final part of his essay on "Rhetoric," Fish attempts to address the claims of inconsistent anti-essentialists, who would try to arrest the "interpretive play" for their own purposes, after exposing the rhetorical nature of all competing claims (596-97, 500-01). Fish presents a more complete version of similar arguments in his essay on "Critical Self-Consciousness" (*DWCN* 436-67), and in his discussion of new historicism (*NSFS* 243-56). Ultimately the argument is the same one that he uses to show that anti-foundationalism will lead to neither the anarchy feared by conservatives, nor the freedom for which liberals hope (*DWCN* 456-59). It all begins to sound very familiar, as Fish once again emphasizes that what makes both options impossible is the primacy of interpretive constraints (inaccessible and inescapable interpretive assumptions). What is particularly curious, however, is the imperatives that arise from Fish's belief in such powerful constraints. On the one hand, because such constraints constitute the inescapable conditions of thought itself, people are not able to avoid holding their own beliefs (including anti-foundationalism) as anything other than universally true (*DWCN* 467, *ITTC* 361-62). At the same time, however, Fish is able to indict those who engage in "anti-foundationalist theory hope," as they reinscribe their own universal claims (*DWCN* 437-38). It turns out that the "inconsistent anti-foundationalists" are only doing what Fish says is inevitable.

We can begin to discern the source of this tension within Fish's argument if we return to that point which we only started to develop earlier, regarding the relative cohesion of the categories in his argument for the primacy of rhetoric. The argument requires, at the very least, that the opposing category of "philosophy" (which includes all belief in mind-independent reality) hang together at least long enough to be subsumed within rhetoric, yet it also requires the maintaining of that opposition upon which that subsuming depends. As a result, Fish's argument depends upon not only equating "belief in the primacy of rhetoric" with every instance of "arguing," but also equating all forms of rational "essentialism" with the Christian belief in a personal God:

> Although the transition from classical to Christian thought is marked by many changes, one thing that does not change is the status of rhetoric in relation to a foundational vision of truth and meaning. Whether the centre of that vision is a personalized deity or an abstract geometric reason, rhetoric is the force that pulls us away from that centre and into its own world of ever-shifting shapes and shimmering surfaces. (*DWCN* 476)

Fish's depiction of the Greek sophists as anti-essentialists may be accurate (*DWCN* 72-73, 480), but by emphasizing the enduring nature of the argument between essentialists and anti-essentialists, Fish also suggests that the differences between Christian and classical thought are simply not relevant to his argument. Although such a gesture may be justified in view of his immediate point, the passage indicates a number of problems which will become evident as we proceed. We can already note two points: first, the anti-rhetorical position is identified using the term "foundational"; second, Fish's ability to group together all positions involving a belief in mind-independent reality depends upon treating the distinction between "personal" and "rational" ("abstract geometric reason") as negligible, or at least irrelevant. Fish could qualify his assertion by pointing out that he is only making the equation within the context of his present argument regarding "rhetoric." However, this same point runs throughout Fish's work: the insistence that his argument does not need to distinguish between a "personalized deity" and "an abstract geometric reason." For example:

> In Andrewes's theology the self is constituted not by a system but by the indwelling presence of Jesus Christ; but the effect of the two ways of think-

ing is the same, to deny the distinction between the knower and the object of knowledge that is so crucial to a positivist epistemology. (*ITTC* 181)

Here Fish again insists that, for the present purposes of his argument at least, there is no need to distinguish between "person" and "system":

> If, as Paul Ricoeur has said, "structuralism is Kantianism without a transcendental subject," then Christianity is structuralism *with* a transcendent subject. This one difference of course makes all the difference. . . .
>
> (*ITTC* 182; original emphasis)

Although Fish qualifies his statement by admitting the significance of the central "difference" between structuralism and Christianity (i.e., theism), such a qualification only serves to emphasize the unqualified status of the implicit premise in his deduction (a premise not required by Ricoeur's generalization): that is, Christianity is the same as Kantianism. This is only one example, but as the previous chapter attempted to show, a large part of Fish's argument in general depends upon this same denial of any important distinction between rationalism and Christianity.

Even if we allow Fish to limit his point to the present argument concerning rhetoric, his position still requires that the category of "anti-rhetorical" must hang together at least long enough to be subsumed within rhetoric. By the criteria of its own implicit assumptions (for the moment there are no others available), the argument will collapse if something escapes the "rhetoric vs. anti-rhetoric" dichotomy. Of course, there is a sense in which Fish is simply pointing out that, regardless of whether people believed in Plato's "Form of the Good" ("abstract geometric reason") or some version of a Christian God who is personal, in both cases, "rhetoric" (as eloquence) was normally regarded with suspicion. Such a generalization, however, no longer holds when "rhetoric" is redefined as the "act of arguing" (disputation) in general. Here again, the shift in his use of terms is crucial, because not all essentialism is inherently distrustful of all "argument" (debate or dialogue) in general. The entire tradition of medieval education (with its emphasis upon oral debate) makes such an assertion untenable. The deeper problem is that insofar as Fish's argument needs to make the notion of "person" reducible to "abstract geometric reason," it depends upon a reinscription of the classical rationalism that it would reject. In order to understand better how this actually happens within Fish's argument, we must first briefly outline some of the ways in which classical science was challenged by early Christian thinking on the Trinity.

By suggesting that the differences between classical and Christian thought are not relevant to the more basic "argument" between rhetoric and philosophy (translated into "anti-essentialism" and "essentialism" respectively), Fish's argument conceals the more basic way in which its own dichotomy depends upon something outside its categories. Classical science was characterized by the search for "*arche* in nature" (*physis*) (Cochrane 362). Of course, there were also those who sought the *arche* "outside" nature, and who consequently ended up with the notion of the "two worlds" (the sensible and the intelligible) (238), but ultimately classical skepticism, materialism and idealism were based in the same initial query. The Platonic division between the realm of "being" and the realm of "becoming," in order to restrict science to the former (238), was only the most successfully universal attempt, among others, to seek the truth of nature (360). Because the sophists (Fish's "rhetoricians") employed the distinction between nature and culture (*physis* versus *nomos/techne*) (Derrida, *Writing* 283) just as the Platonists had, they too participated ultimately in that same classical inquiry into nature. As a result, these various approaches, from the most hopefully ideal to the most radically skeptical, shared in common the treatment of nature as an object of experience. In addition, the most powerful (not necessarily the most immediately popular) among these approaches (i.e., Platonic and Aristotelian) shared in common the belief in a rational order within nature, which was then identified as the supreme good or *prima substantia* (Cochrane 76-81). Ultimately, however, the failure of Platonism resulted from its "inability to overcome the radical deficiencies of the classical approach to experience" (360).[2] Because classical science deduced from nature the supremacy of reason, human "nature" (*psyche* and *polis*) could then be reduced (potentially at least) to reason. This is why I suggested earlier that Fish's argument depends in part upon a reinscription of "classical science," in that it depends upon making "person" equivalent to "reason," so that all "essentialism" can then be labelled "anti-rhetorical." Although Fish rejects essentialism, his argument for that rejection depends upon being able to treat all "essences" as sub-personal. That Fish shares the classical (whether sophist or rationalist) orientation towards nature is apparent even in his choice of the term "personal*ized* deity" (*DWCN* 476; emphasis added), in that he presumes a deity who is "made personal" through anthropomorphic projection. But such a conception of *anthropos* could only be derived from a rational apprehension of nature, so that "person" could always be reduced to rationally mastered components.

What such a grouping (of personal and sub-personal essentialism) overlooks, however, is the way in which early Christian thinking on the Trinity, in attempting to understand the Incarnation, subverted the very categories of classical science. The Incarnation challenged Platonic essentialism because it rejected the notion that the realm of "being" (*esse*) was the exclusive repository of intelligibility—against the sensible realm of becoming (Cochrane 283). More importantly, the reason the trinitarian position was able to maintain a single realm of common human experience (283) was that it did not participate in the attempt to locate a reality principle "inside" or "outside" of nature (362). In this way, trinitarian apprehension of the Incarnation opposed that quest which the sophists (rhetoricians) and philosophers held in common. The attempt to understand revelation led to the insight (noted earlier in Augustine) that "faith is not a substitute for," but "a condition of understanding" (402). "Knowledge of such a principle, therefore, differed *toto caelo* from knowledge of nature; and it was not to be attained by pursuing the chain of natural causation to its limit" (362). The new "question of primary importance [for humans] was not so much their capacity for thinking as the presuppositions which governed their thought" (238). This is why the fourth-century classicists who opposed Christianity could view their conflict (much like modern rationalists) as one between "science and superstition" (402). In contrast, Augustine (and Trinitarians in general), by pointing out the primacy of belief in all knowledge claims, exposed "the great illusion of Classicism" in its pretensions "to apprehend 'objective' truth" (402-03; cf. MacIntyre 99). This resulted from the Christian understanding of "faith" which is placed *in* a Deity who is "not an object of, but a basis for, experience" (238). Here we see the striking parallel between the early Christian insight into the primacy of belief and Fish's poststructuralist argument for the primacy of interpretive assumptions ("faith"). The pivotal difference is that the fourth-century Christian insight into the primacy of belief only developed within a simultaneous apprehension of what the content of that "faith" must be.

Because Fish's argument depends upon the same "naturalist" orientation (in the above sense) shared by both the sophists and the rationalists of classical science, it leads to the same consequences. Earlier we noticed how the last section of Fish's essay on "Rhetoric" attempts to address the "inconsistent anti-essentialists" who reinscribe their own "absolute truth" in the course of exposing someone else's "rhetoric" (*DWCN* 494-502). What Fish's argument demonstrates, however, is that not only is "philosophy" (reason/logic) never completely free from rhetorical considerations, but that even a purely "rhetorical" position is untenable. In effect, "inconsistent anti-essentialism" is the *only* kind of anti-essentialism possible, because the criteria for "consistency" will always be open to challenge from within the anti-essentialist position. There are times when Fish seems to concede this same point, when he argues that people cannot actually live as though their beliefs were not universally true (*ITTC* 360-62; *DWCN* 467). At the same time, his arguments against all "anti-foundationalist theory hope" imply that there is some alternative to inconsistency (*DWCN* 494-501). He insists both that his anti-foundationalism (and all theory) is inapplicable as such, but that the very act of theorizing constitutes its own context of practice. This duality parallels the way that classical science's focus upon nature led to a reduction of psychology to calculation, even as it resulted in a corresponding rejection of such rationalism, because of its failure to account for crucial dimensions of human experience.

Fish's argument for the primacy of rhetoric is, in one sense, very similar to Ong's point that logic has never been successfully separated from rhetoric. An important difference between them, however, is that Fish's argument mistakenly equates all belief in mind-independent truth with a faith in a logic that is independent of rhetoric. Fish's argument simultaneously depends upon and rejects the Ramist separation between rhetoric and "logic" (philosophic objectivism), while making impossible the consideration of any alternative to that dichotomy.[3] Why is it that, from the recognition that presuppositions govern thought, Augustine concludes that it is therefore imperative to have the right presuppositions ("faith"), while Fish concludes that it is therefore impossible to judge which presuppositions are right? It is important to remember that, in reaching his conclusion, Fish adds the insistence that we cannot avoid acting as though it is possible to judge between presuppositions. Obviously this leaves a vast chasm between Fish's account and his own declared experience, and in this respect his argument once again mirrors the crisis of classical science.

Earlier we noted that Fish's attempt to account for temporal reading experience ended up ironically reducing subjectivity to the operation of subpersonal interpretive assumptions. Only now can we begin to see that such a conclusion is in perfect keeping with the attempt to account for temporal experience through "nature" (as *physis*—whether simply sense experience, or a "reality" whose independence is later denied). Yet the question of whether Fish has finally been successful in detaching "rhetoric" (as belief in the primacy of interpretive assumptions) from its metaphysical moorings has only been partially answered. Fish's argument is effective in analyzing any logic which claims independence from all contextual considerations. However, his own "faith" in the primacy of interpretive assumptions (as a faith) remains a surd element, in that it ends up leading to the same problems usually associated with reductive rationalism. We also noted earlier that part of the appeal of Fish's argument results from the sophisticated pragmatism it offers, by insisting that there are no consequences resulting from the abandonment of metaphysics. Given Fish's unsuccessful attempt to extricate rhetoric from philosophy, we must ask whether he has been successful in the attempt to abandon metaphysics:

> There is no sense in doing without the concepts of metaphysics in order to shake metaphysics. We have no language—no syntax and no lexicon—which is foreign to this history; we cannot pronounce a single destructive proposition which has not already had to slip into the form, logic and the implicit postulations of precisely what it seeks to contest.

> To concern oneself with the founding concepts of the entire history of philosophy, to deconstitute them is not to undertake the work of the philologist or of the classic historian of philosophy. Despite appearances, it is probably the most daring way of making the beginnings of a step outside philosophy. The step "outside philosophy" is much more difficult to conceive than is generally imagined by those who think they made it long ago with cavalier ease, and who in general are swallowed up in metaphysics in the entire body of discourse which they have claimed to have disengaged from it.
>
> (Derrida, *Writing* 280-81, 284)

Fish argues that there are no consequences to rejecting metaphysics, but he seems to presume that such a rejection is possible (and complete) in the first place. As a result, our examination of Fish's use of the concepts "faith" and "rhetoric" ultimately leads us to consider more directly the subject of the Trinity. Whether the doctrine of the Trinity is part of that "history of philosophy" described by Derrida (284),[4] or whether it constitutes taking a step in thinking "outside philosophy" (as Fish implies he has done), that doctrine constitutes the central point of difference between Milton and Augustine. It is also one major issue that Fish never addresses directly in his treatment of either writer.

CHAPTER FIVE

Caritas

By subsuming all arguments into his "rhetoric vs. rationalism" dichotomy, Fish obscures any account of the means by which the primacy of interpretive assumptions was first discerned as an alternative to the impasses of classical science. Central to the discernment of that alternative was the development of the doctrine of the Trinity, the God who subsists in a relation of charity. As an attempt to apprehend, in limited human terms, the implications of the Incarnation, the doctrine of the Trinity afforded a unique opportunity to discern the importance of interpretive assumptions in any discursive knowledge claims (see chap. 4). Fish's own argument implicitly claims a transcendence of the very dichotomy that he claims is all-encompassing. However, the trinitarian insight regarding the primacy of faith was not separable from an understanding of what the content of that faith should be, while Fish's account makes the possibility of content inherent to such an insight constitutionally non-specifiable. This is why it is important that Fish's account of Christian hermeneutics, and specifically the rule of charity, omits the doctrine of the Trinity as a central point of disagreement between Milton and Augustine.

As we now turn to examine Fish's evasion of Augustine's teaching on the Trinity, we should note that there are those (e.g., Colin Gunton) who would blame Augustine for the general tendency towards "platonizing" (modalism) in Western theology, and for the excessive rationalism and individualism which has shaped Western understandings of the Trinity. James Doull, however, suggests that the introduction of "an unknowable objective principle" (rationalist modalism) into the Western view of the Trinity came from those who immediately followed Augustine, rather than from Augustine's own teaching (152). I have already (in chap. 3) mentioned the important respects in which Augustine explicitly stated his rejection of Platonism. However, because such charges are still common, before treating directly Fish's handling of Augustine, we shall compare pertinent passages from Descartes, Augustine, and Fish, in order to demonstrate some of the central differences between them. First, Descartes:

But what, then, am I? A cogitating thing. What is that? A thing doubting, understanding, affirming, denying, willing, not willing, also imagining and sensing of course.

These things are indeed many—if they would all pertain to me. But why would they not pertain to me? Is it not now I myself who am now doubting almost all things, who still understand something, who affirm that this one thing is true, deny the other things, desire to know more things, do not want to be deceived, imagine many things even involuntarily, as well as notice many things as coming through my senses? . . . What is there of these things that might be called "separate" from myself? For that it be I who be doubting, who be understanding, who be willing, is so manifest that there might occur to me nothing through which it might be explicated more evidently.
(Descartes 2.8-9)

Now, Augustine:

And one has attempted to establish this and another that. Yet who ever doubts that he himself lives, and remembers, and understands, and wills, and thinks, and knows, and judges? Seeing that even if he doubts, he lives; if he doubts, he remembers why he doubts; if he doubts, he understands that he doubts; if he doubts, he wishes to be certain; if he doubts, he thinks; if he doubts, he knows that he does not know; if he doubts, he judges that he ought not to assent rashly. Whosoever therefore doubts about anything else, ought not to doubt all these things; which if they were not, he would not be able to doubt anything. (Augustine, *On the Trinity* 10.10.14)

The first important difference between these passages is that Augustine is not in the process of locating his epistemic first principles, whereas Descartes, in the parallel quotation, is specifically trying to locate that foundation of certainty (beyond doubt) upon which he can then logically "build" his knowledge—one proposition at a time.[1] We have already noted that Augustine holds no such faith in deduction, because though the rules of inference may be certain, the premises never can be. It is also significant (though not to be overemphasized) that Descartes' exclusive use of the first person singular characterizes an individual thinking in isolation.

What then is Augustine's objective? We must remember that Augustine already understands that all knowledge claims are a function of previously held beliefs, and that as a result he has already placed his trust in the transcendent yet personal creator who is *caritas*, as his existential (rather than proscriptively logical) starting point. The analysis of his own psyche is part of the larger project of "faith seeking understanding." He is using his own mind (memory, will and understanding) as a way of understanding the Trinity, all the while admitting the problems inherent in such attempts at analogy (*On the Trinity* 15.22.42-15.24.44). Augustine's project is then actually the opposite of Descartes', in that Descartes' goal is to establish the certainty of an individual ego which can then successfully master objects in the world, while Augustine is trying to understand (without controlling) the mystery of a transcendent God who is also personal. Furthermore, Augustine's understanding of God (albeit imperfect) is specifically not of a "personalized deity," because his apprehension of "person" is rooted in his faith about and in God. Fish might object that Augustine is simply fooling himself, if he thinks that God, rather than his own sensible experience, provides the basis for his understanding of "person." Such an objection, however, depends upon forgetting that Augustine takes his understanding of "God as person" from the revelation of Christ—the life of *caritas*. As we established in chapter 3, that revelation of "God as person" is itself not learned from a reified text, but from participation in an interpretive community that continues to incarnate a life which subverts the categories of both rationalist essentialism and anti-essentialism.

Each of the above quotations invites comparison with a passage from Fish's *Is There a Text?* Fish's argument is by now familiar, but his choice to engage the same lexicon used by Descartes and Augustine provides an ideal opportunity for parallel reflection:

> Doubting is not something one does outside the assumptions that enable one's consciousness; rather doubting, like any other mental activity, is something that one does within a set of assumptions that cannot at the same time be the object of doubt. That is to say, one does not doubt in a vacuum but from a perspective, and that perspective is itself immune to doubt until it has been replaced by another which will then be similarly immune. . . . To put the matter in a slightly different way: radical skepticism is possible only if the mind exists independently of its furnishings, of the categories of understanding that inform it; but if as I have been arguing, the mind is constituted by those categories, there is no possibility of achieving the distance from them that would make them available to a skeptical inquiry. (*ITTC* 360-61)

As expected, this passage will eventually lead to Fish's oft-repeated point that we cannot hold our own beliefs as though they were not universally true (or belonged to someone else, or were in radical doubt). Rather than try to locate propositions of certitude, Fish points out that even the most radical doubt must presuppose something as certain (though not always the same thing). A critical difference between Augustine and Fish, however, is that Fish is still operating within the rationalist discourse of "propositions" rather than from experience. Of course, Fish destabilizes the rationalist desire for certainty by insisting that we can never know what our most deeply held assumptions are until they are no longer operating as such. Yet Fish still treats the "inaccessible and inescapable" interpretive "constraints" *as* propositions—objects of mastery. Although he insists that we can never view (master) them all at once, there is no basic distinction to be made between those propositions we interrogate as objects before the mind (consciousness) and those propositions ("categories") which constitute the mind. If we look back again at the passage from Augustine, we notice that his focus is rather on experience, and more importantly, that he is not trying to make the experience into a proposition which he can then either "build upon," or use to declare that building is impossible because the "pieces" refuse to hold still. For example, one of the things he mentions is memory: "even if he doubts, he remembers why he doubts." Augustine does not then proceed to use the proposition "I remember" as a basis for sure knowledge (not even "I remember that I forget"). What he will do elsewhere, as in book 10 of the *Confessions*, is reflect on his experience of memory to help him understand who God is and how God deals with people. The key point here is that Augustine requires neither a proposition of logical certainty as does Descartes, nor a proposition of *in*determinacy as Fish does, because his experience is rooted in faith. The object of Augustine's trust (existential "faith in"), however, is not a group of subpersonal interpretive assumptions (inaccessible propositions) but a living God who is revealed in Jesus of Nazareth—the God whose essence (Being) he knows and experiences[2] as *caritas*.

Earlier we noted that Fish's reading of Augustine was directly shaped by his reading of Milton, but that his earlier adoption of Augustine's terms allowed him to attenuate the dependence of his own arguments upon rationalist assumptions. Despite his rhetorical deployment of Augustine, Fish is later able to argue that the "rule of charity" cannot function as an interpretive constraint. This rejection of the rule of charity once again raises the issue of Milton's influence upon Fish, given Milton's anti-trinitarian position.[3] We can now begin to perceive how the primary differences between Milton's and Augustine's view of the Trinity relate to their differing deployments of the principle of reason.

One key point on which Milton's *De Doctrina* differs from Augustine's work by the same name pertains to the relative value of rational understanding over *caritas*.[4] Earlier I observed that Augustine rejected the Platonic tendency to identify rationality or reason itself with the Supreme Good, because of the attendant separation of knowledge from *caritas* (gift-love) and because it encouraged pride (the illusion of self-sufficiency). By contrast, Milton's *De Doctrina* subordinates *caritas* to reason as an interpretive principle. Ostensibly, the general outline of his *De Doctrina* seems to make "charity" the entire concern of book 2. However, Milton quickly reduces Augustine's notion of *caritas* to the modern sense of "charity" (ethical action),[5] and, more importantly, he treats it solely as an object of theological consideration (as a proposition) rather than as a core interpretive principle. We also noted earlier that *De Doctrina* establishes the relation between "faith" and "charity" in such a way that both are functions of how the treatise defines "knowledge of God." Knowledge is then described in such a way that equates reason with the Supreme Good, effectively making formal logic, rather than charity, the primary interpretive constraint. More importantly, because this arrangement then makes "charity" completely dependent upon "knowledge of God" ("faith"), any understanding of charity must, in effect, be constituted by the principles of formal logic:

> [God] cannot do things which, as it is put, imply a contradiction. Accordingly we must remember here that nothing can be said of the one God that is inconsistent with his unity, and which makes him both one and not one. (*CD* 148)

Obviously this point is only the beginning of Milton's argument against the Trinity, but with respect to the qualified sense in which we earlier said that Augustine is not a Platonist, we can already say that Milton clearly *is* to some degree a Platonist, in that his reading of Scripture consistently makes "charity" dependent upon formal logic. Milton's position also helps to explain why Fish can later reject the rule of charity as part of his rejection of "formalism" in general. As also noted earlier, Augustine avoids this problem by recognizing that the truth of logical inference can never guarantee true propositions (*OCD* 2.32.50). How then does Augustine maintain the belief in mind-independent reality without participating in the same rationalist assumptions? In order to begin answering such a question we need to examine directly the differences in their approach to the Trinity.

In discussing Augustine's *De Doctrina*, Fish is careful to observe and cite Augustine's important distinction between "use" and "enjoyment" (*SCA* 24). However, because Fish is primarily interested at that point in supporting his own argument for *Self-Consuming Artifacts,* he implausibly links Augustine's distinction with his own contrast between a "rhetorical" and a "dialectical" presentation:[6]

> To enjoy the things of this world is to have a *rhetorical* encounter with them; to use them is to have a *dialectical* encounter. (*SCA* 24; original emphasis)

We can begin to see some of the problems in Fish's representation of Augustine if we compare Fish's quotation with the fuller passage from Augustine:

> Some things are to be enjoyed, others to be used. . . . Those things which are to be enjoyed make us blessed. (*OCD* 1.3.3 as quoted in *SCA* 24)

> Some things are to be enjoyed, others to be used, and there are others which are to be enjoyed and used. Those things which are to be enjoyed make us blessed. (*OCD* 1.3.3)

At one level, the omission of the third category (of things which are to be *both* enjoyed and used) is understandable because its inclusion would make the passage more difficult for Fish to connect with his own dichotomy of "rhetorical vs. dialectical." In effect, he would have had to complicate his own binary opposition with a third category of "those things which are both rhetorical and dialectical." But the removal of this third category also makes it easier to misconstrue Augustine's position as some kind of reductive functionalism. This oversimplification is important because it indicates part of the basis upon which Fish will later render Augustine's position incoherent.

This shift in terms is the first indication that Fish is actually reorienting Augustine's entire discussion of "use" and "enjoyment." The movement is pivotal because Augustine will later use the term "enjoyment" in defining *caritas*. This development becomes more apparent as we examine Fish's account of Augustine's position regarding what it is that Augustine says we should enjoy:

> The allegory is, of course, commonplace and transparent: our native country is the "better country" of Hebrews XI where we shall enjoy the everlasting bliss of those who move and sing before the lamb; the vehicle is this temporal life and its "amenities," all those things usually referred to as the "pleasures of this world." (*SCA* 24)

This passage is important because it is the very closest that Fish actually comes to stating openly what it is that Augustine insists that we should enjoy. Repeatedly and explicitly Augustine states that that which we should enjoy is the Trinity:

> The things which are to be enjoyed are the Father the Son and the Holy Spirit, a single Trinity. (*OCD* 1.5.5)

94

But if you cling to that delight and remain in it, making it the end of your rejoicing, then you may truly and properly be said to be enjoying it. And this kind of enjoyment should not be indulged except with reference to the Trinity, which is the highest good and is immutable. (1.33.36)

Obviously there is a sense in which Fish is not *completely* "misrepresenting" Augustine's position, in that Fish does generally indicate that "God" is, according to Augustine, the one to be enjoyed. However, given the repeated and explicit emphasis that Augustine places on the Trinity, why does Fish never even mention the Trinity by name? It could be argued that such an oversight or shift in emphasis in Fish's interpretation of Augustine is hardly unreasonable. But this particular shift in emphasis represents a deep misunderstanding of the central issue in Augustine's *De Doctrina*. Later, we shall attend specifically to Milton's argument against the Trinity, but already Fish's neglect of this central point indicates a further respect in which his reading of Augustine has been shaped by Miltonic thinking.

If we return to consider Augustine's initial distinction between use and enjoyment, we can see that the point which he makes is more subtle than Fish's dichotomy between "rhetoric" and "dialectic" would allow. Fish's appropriation of the categories makes it seem that people should only be "used" in some devotionally or spiritually exploitative manner. The key point for Augustine is that there are degrees of "enjoyment," or rather, he refines his terms to distinguish between "enjoyment" as "complete enjoyment," and "enjoyment" as temporal "delight." The latter is not expected to yield "complete happiness" (*OCD* 1.33.36-37). This is why Augustine can distinguish between enjoying (delighting in) other people and finding "complete enjoyment" (*perfrui*) only in God:

> Haec autem merca summa est, et ipso perfruamur et omnes, qui eo fruimur, nobis etiam inuicem in ipso perfruamur.
>
> Nam si in nobis id facimus, remanemus in via et spem beatitudinis nostrae in homine uel in angelo conlocamus. Quod et homo superbus et angelus superbus arrogant sibi atque in se aliorum spem gaudent consititui. (*DDC*, SAA 1.32.35-1.33.36)

> The greatest reward is that we enjoy Him and that all of us who enjoy Him may enjoy one another in him.
>
> For if we find complete enjoyment in ouselves we remain on the road and place our hopes of blessedness in a man or in an angel. Thus the proud man or proud angel places his enjoyment in himself and rejoices that others place their hopes in him also. (*OCD* 1.32.35-1.33.36)

Augustine's point is simple but easy to miss if we depend upon Fish's interpretative dichotomy: while many people and things can be properly enjoyed and loved, humans can find *complete* happiness (*beatitudo*) only in the person of God:

> I call "charity" the motion of the soul toward the enjoyment of God for his own sake, and the enjoyment of one's self and ones neighbor for the sake of God; but "cupidity" is a motion of the soul toward the enjoyment of one's self, one's neighbor, or any corporal thing for the sake of something other than God. (*OCD* 3.10.16)

This is why Augustine describes Christian pilgrimage as travelling on a "road of the affections" (*OCD* 1.17.16) (Poland 46). Once again, it would be easy to render Augustine's position incoherent by imposing upon his terms the rationalist categories of a mastering subject and sub-personal object. His repetition of the term "use," in earlier passages, could then be taken to imply some kind of reductive functionalism. Augustine's ability to assert the mind-independent reality of *caritas* to serve as standard for human action and affection is predicated upon that *caritas* (essence) of God which is constituted by the relationship between the irreducible and indivisible persons of the Trinity. By simplifying Augustine's distinction between "use" and "enjoyment" to fit his own categories of "dialectic" and "rhetoric," Fish is able to avoid completely the core issue of the content of Augustine's "faith" (as both what he believes, and the relationship he trusts).

The *amor* in Augustine's use of the phrase *amor Dei* is not simply "desire," but includes "enjoyment" which rests in God as an end, rather than desiring God as a means to something else (Kroeker 184-85). Augustine's notion of "ordered love" depends not upon a desire for rational order as an end in itself (like Platonism), but upon that restful enjoyment of God who is the end. That enjoyment (*caritas*), which engages nothing less than the entire person, then constitutes the ordering principle of all other loves, desires, uses and enjoyments. The term "order" may be misleading here, because this "ordering of the affections" is not dependent upon formal logic ("the rules of inference"), but provides both a basis and a constraint for reason. For those who would insist that reason needs no such basis or *constraint,* it is necessary only to offer Fish's argument that reason can never escape being the function of some kind of contextual assumptions (*DWCN* 518). Conversely, Fish's argument applies only to rationalist objectivism (which treats reason as an end in itself) and not to Augustine's position, because the enjoyment of God (*caritas*) (engaging the whole person) is not dependent upon a rationalist claim to "a neutral space in the mind," which provides access to an ahistorical objectivity through some psychological "core of rationality" (*DWCN* 517). Fish's use of the term "rationality" is incapable of accounting for a deployment of intelligibility which does not make reason itself the highest good. His repeated point is that reason can never perform the supreme (or objective) function that rationalists claim for it, because it can never be separated from rhetorical (contextual) considerations. Augustine does not participate in the assumptions of modern rationalism because he never separates rationality or his own cognition from the created temporal order, nor does he make reason the supreme good (see chap. 3 above). This is why "Augustine's realism is rooted not only in a 'dramatic-historical mode of apprehension' but also in a 'dramatic-natural' and 'dramatic-rational' theology of creation" (Kroeker 137). The categories of Fish's arguments are incapable of rendering Augustine's position coherently, because all appeals to "reason" or "mind-independent" reality are tacitly converted into the radically "objectivist" assumptions of modern (quasi-Cartesian) rationalism and then explicitly or implicitly dismissed as self-refuting.

In chapter 2 we established some of the ways in which Fish's reading of Augustine had been shaped by his understanding of Miltonic "faith." If we look specifically at Milton's argument against the Trinity, presented in his *De Doctrina Christiana*, we can begin to understand how Fish is able to maintain a belief in such "faith," while insisting that *caritas* cannot provide any constraint upon interpretation. Such an alignment of positions is hardly surprising, given that Milton's rejection of the doctrine of the Trinity results primarily from his subjection of *caritas* to the principle of reason. Milton begins laying the foundation for his argument within his treatment of the doctrine of God. In demonstrating that "God in his most simple nature is a SPIRIT" (*CD* 140), Milton presents five common biblical proof-texts, before proceeding to deduce some rather far-reaching implications:

> From this it may be deduced that the essence of God, since it is utterly simple, allows nothing to be compounded with it, and that the *hypostasis*, Heb. i.3, which is variously translated *substance, subsistence,* or *person,* is nothing but the most perfect essence by which God exists from himself, in himself, and through himself. For neither *substance* nor *subsistence* can add anything to an utterly complete essence and the word *person,* in its more recent use means not the thing itself but the essence of the thing in the abstract. *Hypostasis,* therefore, is clearly the same as essence, and in the passage cited above many translate it by the Latin word *essentia.* Therefore, just as God is an utterly simple essence, so he is an utterly simple substance. (*CD* 140-42)

This passage provides the first premises of Milton's argument against the Scholastic "sophistry" of the Trintarian doctrine (212). In the single step of rejecting any distinction between the terms "essence," "hypostasis" and "substance," Milton has already set himself against the whole of Eastern and Western orthodox tradition. The Cappadocian (Greek) orthodox formulation of the Trinity, for example, depended upon the very distinction which Milton denies (Gunton 42). According to the Cappadocians, "hypostasis" refers specifically "to the concrete particularity of the Father, Son and Spirit," who are "not individuals but persons," "whose reality can only be understood in terms of their relation to each other, relations by virtue of which they constitute the 'being' (*ousia*) of the one God" (42). The Western church has historically had difficulty translating these terms (*hypostasis* and *ousia*), because their Latin equivalents were previously used as synonyms (i.e., *substantia* and *essentia*). As Augustine points out in *De Trinitate*, this why the term *persona* is used rather than *substantia:*

> Dictum est a nostris Graecis una essentia, tres substantiae: a Latinis autem, una essentia vel substantia tres personae; quia sicut jam diximus, nonaliter in sermone nostro, id est, Latino, essentia quam substantia solet intelligi.
>
> (*De Trinitate* 7.4.7)

> Our Greek friends have spoken of one essence but three substances, but the Latins of one essence or substance, three persons; because as we have already said, essence usually means nothing other than substance in our language, that is, Latin. (*On the Trinity* 7.4.7; Haddan trans.)

The Greek formulation depended upon a distinction between these terms which simply did not exist in their Latin equivalents (in effect, *hypostasis* had a lexical range in Greek which *substantia* did not have in Latin). Milton is able to ignore the distinction between the Greek terms by reversing the historical relationship, effectively arguing that, since the Latin terms are synonymous, so the Greek terms must have been. That the Western church had found it necessary to translate "hypostasis" as "person," rather than "substance," demonstrates the inaccuracy in Milton's claim that "hypostasis," "essence" and "substance" (in reference to God) are equivalent.[7]

As Milton continues his treatment of the doctrine of God, he presents a list of those attributes pertaining to God's nature, which culminates in the ninth and final point, "that God is ONE" (*CD* 146). Milton takes this attribute to be, "as it were, the logical conclusion of them all" (146). Taken alone, the scriptural declaration that God is "one" is in perfect keeping with the orthodox insistence that God is not divisible (that is, triune not tripartite). However, Milton specifically notes (three times) that God is "numerically one" (147), emphasizing the equation of "number" with "essence" which he establishes in his *Artis Logicae* (*AL* 233) (Campbell, "Son" 508). At that point in *De Doctrina*, the foundation of his argument against the Trinity is effectively complete: essence is always equal to number and synonymous with hypostasis and substance; the Trinity, composed of one essence yet three hypostases, is a contradiction and, therefore, false. It is not necessary even to reach the fifth chapter on "The Son," because the Son must already, by implication, be a different essence from the Father, who is numerically one. Because the argument is logically independent, all citations of Scripture after that point are superfluous to the argument against the Trinity. The primary reason Milton must continue to cite Scripture to support his position is that he must still re-interpret the usual trinitarian proof-texts by applying his definitions and logic to those verses (e.g., *CD* 238 ff., esp. 248).

Although Milton rejected the doctrine of the Trinity, he claimed to accept the doctrine of the Incarnation (*CD* 419-20). This is an anomalous position in view of the fact that historically the primary purpose of the doctrine of the Trinity has been to safeguard a thoroughly biblical view of the Incarnation (Erickson 322-38; Strong 313-15, 349-50). Initially, it seems that Milton is simply applying the criterion of *sola scriptura:* he notes that although the doctrine of the Incarnation contradicts his logical principles (holding that two essences [divine and human] can form one person), he accepts the teaching on the basis of scriptural authority (420, 423). However, because he has already demonstrated that the Son cannot be co-essential with the Father, Milton can only use the term "Incarnation" to indicate that Christ is somehow "divine," but not "supreme God" (424-25). Therefore, notwithstanding his apparent acceptance of the authority of Scripture, the shape which Milton gives the doctrine of the Incarnation is still determined by his rationalist first principles. As a result, he is able to use the term "Incarnation" to indicate a "divine human," but not "God in the flesh."

Milton scholars have debated the extent to which Milton actually subordinates the Son, and whether his position in the *De Doctrina* is truly "Arian" (e.g., Campbell 507n; Shullenberger 266-67n; Rumrich 40-49), but regardless of how we classify Milton's argument, his position is openly anti-Trinitarian and is largely a function of his Ramist logic. In keeping with that Ramist method, Milton's chapter on the Son proceeds by multiplying the logical subdivisions of his topic. After treating the divisions of "internal efficiency," Milton divides the "external efficiency" of God into GENERATION, CREATION, and THE GOVERNMENT OF THE UNIVERSE" (*CD* 205), arguing that the generation of the Son is external to the essence (being) of God, because generation implies an event external to the Father. Within orthodox thinking, the generation of the Son is indeed external to the Father, but internal to the essence of the triune God. Milton is able to refute this logically by equating "God" exclusively with "Father," and then arguing that any generation from the Father must, therefore, be external to God. Once again, Milton simply re-applies the same basic definitions and logical inferences regarding the essential (numeric) unity and simplicity of God. Although he cites multiple passages of Scripture which mention the role of Christ in creation (206), he draws from them precisely the opposite conclusion that Trinitarians draw from the same verses. Milton concludes that "all these passages prove that the Son existed before the creation of the World, but not that his generation was from eternity" (206). In the only three passages within the *De Doctrina* where Milton cites John 1:3 (Bauman 104), he never quotes the second half of the verse: "and without him nothing was made that has been made." By arguing that the Son is created, Milton contradicts this scriptural assertion that the Son is not created, and thereby denies that the Son is the one creator God. If all things came into being through the Son, such that he is the exclusive means of divine making, the *logos* must be uncreated (Augustine, *Homilies* 10).[8] According to Milton's own categories, there can be only one who is the infinite, eternal creator. As a result, Milton contradicts not only Scripture but his own logic when he concludes,

> So God begot the Son as a result of his own decree. Therefore it took place within the bounds of time, for the decree itself must have preceded its execution. (*CD* 209)

Given that Milton has already agreed that all creation exists only through the Son (206), this conclusion involves a surprisingly obvious logical contradiction, by implying that time is uncreated and therefore eternally self-existent (cf. Augustine, *Conf.* 262-63). Although the logic of Milton's argument against the Trinity finally contradicts *both* Scripture *and* his own rationalist first principles, his conclusion is most important because of what it implies regarding both the nature of God and human access to God.

In arguing that the generation of the Son results from God's "external efficiency" (*CD* 205), Milton cannot avoid also making that *caritas* which constitutes their relationship external to God's essence (being). Milton is consistent with this deduction, in his earlier presentation of the "Doctrine of God." In listing the nine "attributes which represent God's nature" (*CD* 139-49), he makes no mention of God's love (*caritas*). Only in the list of those attributes "which show his divine power and excellence" (*DDC*, IM 55) do we find any mention of God's love. Under the heading of "God's will" and the sub-heading "he is MOST GRACIOUS [SUMME BENIGNUS]" (*DDC*, IM 56-57) we find one citation of 1 John 4:8 (*Deus est caritas*) (*DDC*, IM 58). In this way, Milton never even formally treats *caritas* as an attribute of God's "efficiency" (not to mention God's essence), and places himself in direct opposition to the orthodox understanding that God's indivisible essence is constituted by *caritas*. Even if we grant the extent to which Milton does admit the description of God as a "loving" monad, because God's essence does not consist of a love relationship, the essential difference between God and Christ would still leave that monadic love inaccessible to humans. Milton could still talk about Christ's sacrificial death as evidence of God's "love," but that love could never be apprehended as God's essence (being). Instead, because numerical unity is treated as an end in itself, Milton cannot finally avoid identifying arithmetic consistency with God's essence.

Once again, this is not simply a case of Milton "fine-tuning" his doctrine of God. *Caritas* has also dropped out of the *De Doctrina* as an interpretive constraint. The interpretive shift is most apparent in cases where Milton explicitly chooses to view a given passage figuratively (remember that was the primary point of application for Augustine's rule):

> All these passsages prove that the Son existed before the creation of the World, but not that his generation was from eternity. The other texts which are cited indicate only metaphorical generation. (*CD* 206)

Why does Milton choose to interpret these verses metaphorically? He must do so in order to be consistent with his argument thus far that the Son is not eternal, and the determining factor is the logically consistent application of his definitions (categories): not *caritas*. Milton makes this same choice throughout his argument against the Trinity.

Given the earlier noted opposition (in chap. 4) between the rationalism of classical science and the trinitarian view that all such claims to objectivity were only enabled by different beliefs, it is hardly surprising that the most basic opposition to the doctrine of the Trinity came from those who maintained the primacy of classical science. In keeping with this expectation, Arius was openly associated with "Philo, Origen and the Neoplatonists" (Cochrane 234). Milton's *De Doctrina* follows this tradition and as such endorses the methods of rationalist science (ancient and modern) over revelation (in spite of his disclaimers). There is a sense in which the very core of the trinitarian debate turns on the question of whether it is possible to "comprehend the divine nature in terms of arithmetic" (233). The tendency to do so consistently results in either modalism (making the Son one "function" of the divine monad) or else Arianism (making the Son less than "God incarnate"—i.e., created in time) (233):

> From [the trinitarian] standpoint, the distinctions fundamental to the [classical] scientific outlook simply disappeared. For, as the source of Being, this principle was not to be apprehended "objectively"; it eluded analysis in terms of substance, quantity, quality, and relation, all the categories in short which yield a knowledge of the phenomenal world. But, although not cognizable as an object, it was not therefore reducible to terms merely of subjective feeling, for its reality was presupposed in all the manifestations of conscious life, of speculative as well as practical activity. (363)

We can now begin to distil some conclusions which will have a direct bearing on our broader view of Fish's argument. The doctrine of the Trinity not only gives a corrective to the tendency of classical science to anthropomorphize deity, but also ensures that because the notion of "person" (as *imago Dei*) is not reducible to "abstract geometric reason," it guards against the subpersonal view of human nature which follows from making the principle of reason the supreme good. This is why Fish's argument depends upon treating all belief in mind-independent reality as "rationalism," or "essentialism," or "foundationalism," and why such treatment is so deeply mistaken. Because his "rhetoric" is no less dependent than "philosophy" upon the same classical inquiry into "nature," Fish can only maintain the division between the two by equating a supreme rational truth with a personal God. This is why his attempt to sustain the totalizing division between rhetoric and philosophy obscures a possible alternative to the inquiry into nature (*physis*). Fish learns from Milton that *caritas* is always debatable (ineffective as a constraint), because *De Doctrina* subsumes charity within the principle of reason, in effect leaving Platonism in theological garb and excluding *caritas* from God's essence. We can now examine the implications of these conclusions for our understanding of Fish's argument.

Earlier I noted the tension between the way in which Fish's arguments consistently require the maintenance of a Ramist dichotomy between rhetoric and dialectic, and the way that Fish is explicitly opposed to the "spatial" logic of Ramism because it fails to account for the temporal experience of understanding (reading/interpreting). Yet in spite of Fish's declared opposition to objectivism, there is another sense in which his arguments share a deep affinity with Ramism because of their shared "textualist" orientation. Although Fish is consistent in treating rhetoric as an oral phenomenon (using the idioms of auditory discourse), his ability to characterize the debate as being "between rhetorical and foundationalist thought" (*DWCN* 482), and to align Derrida with the "rhetorical" side of the debate (491-94), shows that Fish is still operating within the textualist assumptions which treat word and script as a seamless rhetorical whole. The evidence that such textualist assumptions reach to very heart of Fish's position is that he would make no distinction between the statements "everything is textual" and "everything is rhetorical." When Fish initially set out to overcome formalism by developing the notion of "literature in the reader(s)," and focusing on temporal experience (*SCA* 387-88; *ITTC* 167), he still employed the structuralist assumption that text (inscription), word and world were all basically the same. In spite of his insistence that "the objectivity of the text is an illusion" (*SCA* 400), as his argument developed it still depended upon everything being "textual." Fish could not move coherently from the assertion that "the objectivity of the text is an illusion," to the conclusion that *all* perception of objectivity is an illusion, unless he had already assumed that everything is textual. If not everything is textual then not all perceptions of mind-independent reality are "constructed." This is where Ong's reading of Fish proves incomplete, in that Ong approvingly cites the above quotation from Fish regarding the status of the text, and suggests that reader-response theory could be improved by being made to account for "primary orality" (Ong, *Orality* 171).[9] Ong does not examine the way in which Fish's position radically destabilizes any notions of "fact" upon which the conception of "primary orality" could ever be based. However, Ong's analysis of the relation between Ramism and the development of textualist discourse helps us to see more clearly why reader-response theory is finally incapable of engaging the very issues that Ong suggests it might.

Because he takes the usual poststructuralist position that "everything is textual," Fish cannot avoid making his argument dependent upon the same textualist suppression of all distinction between the diachronic experience of the oral word and the spatial organization of inscription. The failure to make such a distinction contradicts the stated purpose of Fish's initial project in trying to account for temporal reading experience in a way that formalism does not. Although he denies the objectivity of "the text," Fish still treats the "word" primarily as an internalized inscription, and that is why his argument still ends up being quasiformalist (reductive) in his treatment of the interpretive diachronic process. Ultimately both Milton's and Fish's accounts of temporal experience are self-refuting (rather than merely self-consuming) because they depend upon a primarily propositional view of human apprehension. As noted, even Fish's argument against foundationalism still depends upon a belief in the primacy of inaccessible assumptions (propositions). This is why consciousness for Fish is finally reducible to a collection of shifting assumptions. This is also why both Milton's and Fish's subsuming of *caritas* within reason ends up snagged on the problem of time. In Milton's case, his argument subverts itself by inadvertently making time uncreated. In Fish's case, the attempt to account for temporal reading experience finally results in a position which declares its own inapplicability to any temporal experience, because it has reduced consciousness to a complex of assumptions. Neither Fish nor Milton (in *De Doctrina*) ever abandons the primacy of propositions as the basic mode of apprehension.

Augustine's treatment of time in the *Confessions* differs importantly from that of Fish, in that Augustine begins with inter-personal reality and ends up making the idea of "time" itself a function of personal human experience (11.27). This is effectively the reverse of Fish's position which begins by attempting to reject formalism, because of its failure to account for subjectivity, but ends up reinscribing a reified notion of subjectivity (via interpretive assumptions) in trying to account for temporal experience. We can now turn more directly to the question of why, given the agreed primacy of belief, Augustine should conclude that it is therefore imperative to have right beliefs while Fish concludes that it is impossible to determine which beliefs should be consciously chosen. The key difference is that, according to Fish, we can never trust (believe) anything more than assumptions (which may or may not be objectifiable at any given moment), while for Augustine the ultimate object of faith (even in the case of historical testimony) is always irreducible personhood. Augustine is less concerned with belief *about* God than he is with belief *in* God: believing *in* God involves trust (which can involve propositions) but also a "cherishing" of the other (Gilson 31). Therefore *caritas* can function as an interpretive constraint, if "faith" is understood in relation to persons who are not reducible to their assumptions. This involves neither a claim to complete "objectivity," nor a concession to radical subjectivism.

Throughout this argument, I have attempted to show that these two extreme positions (objectivism and subjectivism) are mutually dependent and that neither bears a direct relation to Augustine's position, because he "begins" (a life of faith existentially, not a series of propositions) with the recognition of a mind-independent reality who is not sub-personal. This is why Augustine understood the doctrine of the Trinity as inextricably connected with the ability of *caritas* to provide a constraint on interpretation that does not participate in the aporias of the subject/object dichotomy. This is also why the insight into the primacy of belief did not result in paralysis (become "inconsequential") for Augustine. His insight only emerged within an understanding that the personal God who is *caritas* could be the only worthy object of complete trust.

The most persistent difficulty in trying to give a balanced presentation of Augustine's position in relation to that of Fish is that Fish's theory is so textualist in orientation that its terms of reference cannot avoid distorting Augustine's account. Fish always treats "interpretation" as something akin to a written pronouncement resulting from the operations of certain assumptions which generate a text or recognizable "construing" of some kind. As noted, even when Fish is not talking about texts as such, he treats everything as though it were textual. For Augustine, exegesis is not always the most relevant interpretive act, because *caritas* is not primarily textual. When Saint Paul characterizes *agape* (*caritas*) (1 Cor. 13) as patient, kind, not boastful, not proud and not envious, he makes clear the non-textual nature of *caritas*, and Augustine is consistent with this characterization. There is a sense in which reading well does involve a basic gesture of attentive good will toward another person, what George Steiner calls "*cortesia*" or "tact of heart" (155). However, while it may be possible to exhibit some of the qualities of *caritas* through reading, or through spoken or written exegesis, its full expression encompasses a range of possible actions far beyond the scope of such textual modes. This openness is a vulnerability, permitting Fish to address any given argument (usually in writing), by pointing out that either *caritas* is such a "flabby" category that it can be taken to mean anything, or else it is just another fallacious appeal to objective rationalism. The textualist orientation of Fish's arguments allows him to represent as incoherent anything that does not share his orientation. As we have already established, because Fish's arguments only recognize the categories of either rationalist objectivism or anti-essentialism, he can only read an appeal to *caritas* either as a (false) claim to a rationalist "objective" constraint, or as an admission that there is no mind-independent reality (text) at all.

This double indictment of *caritas* involves a curious set of reversals in Fish's argument. On the one hand, the rule of *caritas* is initially dismissed as a totalizing system; on the other hand, it is dismissed for its complete failure to constrain interpretation. Although interpretive constraints in general are impossible to avoid, the one thing which will not provide a constraint is the rule of *caritas*. All interpretive constraints are simply engines of their own transformation, yet it is imperative that Fish consistently argue against the possibility of transcendent reality (geometric or personal) as an interpretive constraint:

> This [anti-essentialism] does not mean that a notion like "truth" ceases to be operative, only that it will always have reference to a moment in the history of inquiry rather than to some God or material objectivity or invariant calculus that underwrites all our inquiries. (*DWCN* 322)

We have already noted the myriad of problems that are implicit in passages like this and upon which Fish's broader position still depends: treating all transcendent reality as subpersonal, the reductive account behind his idea of "history," and so forth. The key point here is that this passage is typical of Fish's work, in that it disallows all appeals to transcendence. Despite his treatment of a wide range of positions, from materialist linguistic formalism to "anti-foundationalist theory hope," and despite his insistence that we cannot avoid holding our own beliefs as anything other than universally true, the implicit and persistent imperative is that people must not appeal to some transcendent reality. "Must not" may sound too strong, but Fish's argument removes the distinctions between "must not," "need not" and "cannot" (once again we meet the tyranny of interpretive assumptions). It may seem more appropriate to say that Fish simply thinks transcendence to be untenable. Yet, if we remember that "everything is rhetorical," his rejection of transcendence can itself never mean anything more than that appeals to transcendent reality are somehow "not fair" rhetorically.

At this point, one further qualification is in order. In pointing out the differences between my reading of Augustine and Fish's reading of Augustine, I am not simply setting the assumptions of one interpretive community ("Miltonists") against the assumptions of another ("Augustinians"). If that were the case, Fish could simply argue that he is participating in the assumptions of an interpretive community which is different from that of the "Augustinian" reader of the present argument. Such a point is moot, however, because according to Fish's own argument concerning interpretive communities, insofar as the present argument is even intelligible as an argument in relation to his position, it already participates in certain shared assumptions which constitute an interpretive community still broader than "readers of Augustine or Milton." More importantly, to construe the argument as one between two interpretive communities is to conceal how the very notion of the primacy of interpretive assumptions is itself dependent upon the same interpretive assumptions used by Fish to read Augustine. To point out the interpretive assumptions in Fish's reading does not entail that we subscribe to a belief in the primacy of interpretive assumptions, any more than the use of argument necessitates a belief in the primacy of rhetoric. Even within Fish's argument, however, it is possible to talk about those assumptions which are mutually accessible (whether they be points of agreement or disagreement). The present analysis has focused on these "mutually accessible premises" throughout, because, according to Fish's own argument, such assumptions are the only ones which could ever be the object of anyone's conscious thought. This is why, having turned consistently to the issue of Augustine's rule of *caritas*, we are now in a position to bring this recovered Augustinian apprehension of *caritas* into direct engagement with Fish's recent work on professional literary interpretation.

CHAPTER SIX

Teloi

We are now reaching the final stages in our analysis of Fish's ongoing appropriation of Augustinian and Miltonic theological discourse. We have thus far traced some of the main actions that culminated in his conversion to belief in the primacy of interpretive assumptions. Only after that conversion did he apparently discover that such an insight has in itself no consequences, either within a formalized context of practice where a deeper set of assumptions (than the formal ones) always already operate, or in any other context. The inapplicability of his discovery results from the fact that each person is always already embedded in a context of practice. Thus his argument does not lead to inaction or despair because the inapplicability is itself inapplicable—local practices are always already in place. In his most recent monograph, *Professional Correctness,* Fish uses the name "constructivism" to designate that inapplicable belief in the primacy of interpretive assumptions, even as he continues to deploy theological modes of discourse to defend his position. However, we can now begin to see more precisely how such a rhetorical approach risks reinscribing the kind of reductive formalism that Fish initially set out to overcome in *Self-Consuming Artifacts.* Indeed, in his deployment of theological discourse emptied of its ostensible content Fish (like so many practicioners of allegedly postmodern discourse) actually perpetuates one of the most cherished dreams of the same modernity that he purports to oppose. Central to the larger project of Enlightenment rationalism was the attempt to purge theology of its doctrinal specificities ("mythical accretions") and to discover the universal form that shapes all creeds. Although Fish explicitly eschews all "universalism," he seems in his more recent arguments (as we shall see) to be much more accepting of formal strategies. The prospect of such formalism raises the question of whether the traveller has indeed returned to the place of his journey's beginning only to find himself, as well as the place, transformed.

Because the investigation here has specifically traced, among the changes in Fish's position, his shifting rhetorical deployment of

Augustine's rule of charity, as well as the notion of "faith," it may be objected that the present argument is only a rhetorical analysis, given that Fish's appropriation of the rule of charity is simply a rhetorical gesture. "Is it not the case," we might ask, "that Fish's ostensible arguments (at least for constructivism *per se*) could be offered without any reference to Augustine or Milton?" One problem with such a question is that within Fish's own position, rhetorical anlysis is the *only* kind of discursive analysis possible. More importantly, the binary character of his argument used to support his broader position depends upon subsuming Augustine's position within his formalist/anti-formalist dichotomy. This allows Fish to obscure the possibility of an alternative to that binary opposition even while his own implicit claim to transcendence of that dichotomy conceals its dependence upon Augustine as a model. The excavations undertaken by the present argument thus far have therefore also demonstrated the potential for the rule of *caritas* to offer an alternative to Fish's account, specifically because that alternative is drawn out from within the terms of his own analysis. Consequently, as we now trace the narrative trajectory of his position in *Professional Correctness*, his earlier argument's self-disclosure of *caritas* as a possible alternative permits a more direct interrogation of his position with respect to that virtue. In this way, our inquiry still ultimately proceeds from drawing out the possibilities inherent within Fish's own arguments. As we examine the central argument of *Professional Correctness*, we can move toward a direct engagement between Fish's constitutionally contentless "faith in faith" and the Augustinian apprehension of *caritas* that Fish's account would otherwise suppress.

What is most striking about the central argument of *Professional Correctness* is that it could be so easily interpreted as a repudiation of Fish's previously held positions. In fact, he highlights his anxiety over the possibility of such misinterpretation in the final comments of the Preface:

> I would like to provide this book with two directions for the user. 1. Do not read it as evidence that I have changed my mind or my politics. 2. Do not read it as a repudiation of cultural studies, black studies, feminist studies, gay and lesbian studies and other forms of activity that have reinvigorated the literary scene. The argument that unfolds here is absolutely consistent with arguments that I have made since the late 1970's. (*PC* x)

Indeed, because of the consistency between the arguments of *Professional Correctness* and Fish's arguments since the late 1970's (i.e., circa *Is There A Text?*), the more recent work contains few surprises. The main thrust of his argument throughout the book is that "social constructivism" (a.k.a. the primacy of interpretive assumptions), as an argument, has no consequences if it is applied consistently to everything. His basic point is twofold: first, all interpretive or literary "work" (effectiveness) is only constituted as such within the terms of professional disciplinary tasks; second, "simply *announcing* the thesis of social constructedness" does nothing to subvert or further those specific disciplinary goals—constructivism *per se* has no professional or extra-professional consequences (*PC* x). The character of his argument thus requires the above quoted disclaimer because it is precisely such "non-traditional scholarship in the humanities" which typically tries to use constructivism in order to make extra-professional claims; that is, the claim to be doing "political" work. All this by now sounds very familiar. However, Fish insists that his argument does not entail a repudiation of non-traditional scholarship because he does not question the "accomplishments" of such scholarship ("which are many"). Instead, he limits his criticism to "the [political] claims that sometimes accompany those accomplishments" (x). Fish's qualification therefore depends upon the view that the political claims of such non-traditional interpretations are not integral to their professional practice. But such an assertion is simply untenable. If, for example, racial-studies or gender-studies critics ceased to believe that their political criticism of literature had political consequences, they would cease to practice such interpretation. The claim to political effectiveness by such non-traditional criticism is not peripheral but integral to its entire undertaking. It is therefore disingenuous for Fish to suggest that he can leave the "core" of such criticism unchallenged, even while he attacks its claim to do political work. At another level, Fish insists that *Professional Correctness* is consistent with arguments he has made since the late 1970's, but he does not consider that the arguments he has been making since the late 1970's may be inconsistent with themselves. Although he may be correct to insist that his politics have not changed, we need to ask whether his own arguments may have entailed a rejection of those politics from the very beginning. Before we address such a question, however, we need to highlight three ways in which *Professional Correctness* does entail a continuation of Fish's earlier work.

First, lest his argument be pre-emptively dismissed by cultural studies practitioners, we need to clarify how Fish is using the term "political," and how it is consistent with his earlier arguments. When he denies that literary criticism has political consequences, he uses "political" in the "usual" narrow sense to indicate "actions performed with the intention of winning elections or influencing legislators" (50). The more general sense in which cultural studies critics commonly employ the term "politics," to indicate that "every action is ultimately rooted in a contestable point of origin," Fish maintains is so general that it is trivial (50)—in the same way that constructivism universally applied has no consequences. To say that literary criticism is "political" (or rhetorical, or debatable) in this broader sense is to assert something so banal as to be without content because everything is political in that sense. Fish is more than willing to admit that literary interpretations have political consequences in such a general sense, because interpretations clearly do effect changes in professional politics, but precisely not in the realms of electoral or legislative politics. He therefore insists upon using "politics" in the narrower sense, arguing that there is nothing inherent to literary interpretation that excludes it from political (i.e., directly electoral or legislative) influence, but that no institutional structures presently exist in North America whereby such influence can be exerted (93-98). His more important point, however, is that the interpretation of literature is not inherently "political" (in the narrow sense).

This specific use of the term "political" helps to support a much larger point. Once again, as in *Doing What Comes Naturally* and *There's No Such Thing as Free Speech*, Fish rejects both the new historicist claim to do political work through criticism and the conservative opposition to specialized professional literary activity. At one point, he takes Alan Sinfield and Blair Worden as examples of those two respective positions:

> From my perspective Sinfield and Worden are in the same line of work; both want to get beyond the current professionalization of literary studies to something else, to radical political work in Sinfield's case and to the celebration of the texts that embody and preserve our highest values in Worden's case. They are political, and even politically correct, albeit in different directions. I am *professionally* correct, not out of a sense of moral obligation or choice of values—there is no moral dimension to my position at all (I am not urging a practice, but reporting on the imperatives built into a practice), and certainly no choice—but out of a sense that the structure of a fully articulated profession, be it negligence law or literary criticism, is such that those who enter its precincts will find that the basic decisions, about where to look, what to do, and how to do it, have already been made. (*PC* 43-44)

It should be immediately apparent that the "reporting" stance adopted by Fish in this passage is simply a temporary rhetorical pose which he has already declared untenable, according to his own account of the impossibility of "value-free" description. More importantly, the twofold opposition that he describes will lead eventually to Fish's repeated double observation that both the hopes of new historicists and the fears of conservatives are unfounded. The substitution of "partisan political agendas for the decorums of standards of thought proper to the academy" (what is respectively hoped for and feared) will always already be constrained and constituted by professional disciplinary criteria (51-52). Disciplinary intelligibility for literary interpretation precludes the possibility of extradisciplinary consequences because of the way that literary studies are presently constituted. We need not recount in detail the argument that Fish offers to support this (by now familiar) point, but we should note that his refutation of *both* positions depends, as we shall see, upon his argument against the efficacy of "critical self-awareness," particularly the awareness claimed by new historicism (50-52) or cultural studies (104). Fish points out that the hope of cultural studies practitioners is predicated on privileging an *awareness* of one's own contextual embedding, as though that awareness itself somehow enabled the means to escape professional constraints (104). The root problem with such thinking is that "either reflection [concerning a given practice] is the extension of a practice and can claim no distance from it or it is itself a practice and has no privileged relationship to, or even necessary significance for, practices other than itself" (107). Thus, neither the conservative fears nor the new historicist hopes will ever be realized, as professional practice continually evolves. Once again, this mode of argument is consistent with Fish's previous analyses, but the key point is that his arguments for the unavoidable constraints of professional correctness are always aimed (in binary fashion) at one of these two opposing positions and that those arguments depend upon the professional inefficacy of critical self-awareness.

A second important characteristic of *Professional Correctness* is that its arguments continue Fish's established practice of offering a literary interpretation whose ostensible content is independent of his main argument. That is, to challenge the particulars of his given textual interpretation would actually make no difference to his larger arguments about the nature of professional or disciplinary constraints. For example, the first chapter offers a detailed analysis of the first three words of Milton's *Lycidas*, "Yet once more" (*PC* 3-13): however, the real goal, or *telos*, of the analysis is not to prove anything about the poem *per se*, but to demonstrate "yet once more" that literary or interpretive understanding comes "not from the text, which acquires its generic shape and particular details only in the light of that [pre-existing] knowledge," but "from the fact of my [Fish's] embeddedness (almost embodiment) in a field of practice that marks its members with signs that are immediately perspicuous to one another" (16). Although the specific text chosen for explication is not crucial, the nature of Fish's argument does require that his "proof" be exemplified because it can never be stated explicitly (15-16). Fish realizes that to state a defense of professional literary activity in explicit terms would contradict his own argument against the possibility or efficacy of critical self-awareness—a point which, as we shall see, is itself the core of his larger argument for the professionally limited nature of all literary interpretation.

The third notable point of consistency between *Professional Correctness* and Fish's earlier work is that he continues (specifically in the first and last main chapters) to invoke the notion of "faith" (from Hebrews 11) as interpreted through a conflation of Augustinian and Miltonic theological discourse. In fact, the first chapter basically reenacts the central steps of *Is There a Text in This Class?* with gestures toward each of his favorite *topoi*. The central difference between the two performances is that the more recent version more effectively obscures any connection between the theological discourse and his own position: there is only the suggestion of influence by parallel resonance. We see this, for example, when the discussion of Milton's use of the divergent pastoral traditions leads to a full explanation of the contrast between "carnal" and "eschatological" understandings of time:

> [In eschatological time] God's message is manifest no matter who speaks. Intention is not a property of limited consciousness but of the spirit that makes of them an involuntary vehicle. (11)

The direct parallel between this account of "divine intention" and Fish's later argument for the unavoidability of disciplinary constraints (interpretive assumptions) is never pointed out, but shapes his argument in two ways: first, the resonance between the two ideas helps to create the impression that his larger argument about inescapable professional constraints actually depends upon his interpretation of Milton's poem (which it does not, except as one among innumerable possible examples he could have used); second, the parallel is never stated explicitly, allowing Fish to continue obscuring how his position is basically a secularized version of the theological position. But all of this is, of course, technically irrelevant, because the discussion of "eschatological time" is part of an interpretation of *Lycidas* the function of which is precisely not to prove anything about *Lycidas,* but to embody a set of practices whose existence and operation are not susceptible to explicit discursive treatment. Once again, the key interpretive moments from *Self-Consuming Artifacts* and *Is There a Text?* are fully operative. However, there has been one important, though slight, shift. The "transcendent reality" of the earlier accounts, that toward which the self-consuming artifacts gesture (even as they fail to contain it within their forms, etc.), has been replaced by a set of embodied professional practices. In effect, the gods of agnosis, the inescapable yet inaccessible assumptions, have become flesh and are dwelling among us as professors of literature. Nevertheless, we need not fear messianic pretensions, as Fish makes it clear that neither the practitioners nor the practices can save anyone.

The last main chapter of *Professional Correctness*, before the concluding "Coda," is entitled, "Why Literary Criticism is Like Virtue." In that chapter Fish draws together all three of the elements that we have discussed thus far: the main argument against the political consequences of literary criticism, the deployment of textual analyses whose support for that main argument is only incidental, and the continued use of Augustinian and Miltonic discourse as a source for analogues. The first of these is the central argument of the entire collection of lectures, but his deployment of the other two elements in support of his central point has revealing consequences for that larger argument.

In the first part of the chapter, the primary focus of Fish's argument is to refute the claim made by cultural studies practitioners that they are directly changing political reality. He openly admits the existence of "'trickle down' consequences that may or may not flow from the fact that generations of young adults pass through [literary critics'] classrooms"; however, such limited changes "will not be sufficient for those who want to participate in 'the revolutionary transformation of social relations all at one go'" (98). In order to overcome these disciplinary or professional limitations, cultural studies practitioners try to have it both ways: they admit their own contextually constrained position (that the "escape from ideology" is an illusion), but they then valorize the *awareness* of that situatedness, as though the awareness itself enabled them somehow to gain freedom from those ideological constraints (101-02):

> The critically self-conscious agent, the [cultural studies] argument goes, is just as embedded as anyone else, but he is aware of it and that makes all the difference, or at least the difference that keeps the hope of boundary breaking behaviour alive. This will work, however, only if the knowledge that we are embedded is stored in a part of the mind that floats free of the embeddedness we experience at any one time; but that would mean that at least part of our mind was not somewhere but everywhere and that would mean we were not human beings but gods. In a frankly religious tradition the internalization of deity is not only possible, it is obligatory; but in the militantly secular tradition of the new historicism and cultural studies, what is

114

internalized are the routines and deep assumptions of human practices which resemble deity only in that they are jealous of rivals and say to us "Thou shalt have no other gods before me." (104)

I have quoted this passage at length because it offers a brief version of Fish's critique of critical self-awareness in his own words, but also because it demonstrates a classic instance of how he transposes the quandaries of epistemic tribalism into the discourse of Mosaic law. The shift in terms is very useful because it enables Fish to employ an implicit rhetorical indictment of cultural studies in terms of "idolatry," without ever positing his own "absolute," upon which a genuine charge of that kind would necessarily depend. His use of religious terms allows him to suggest that, by claiming the transcendance implicit in valorizing critical self-awareness, cultural studies practitioners betray their own radically immanent god of secular constructivism.

By claiming to escape "the grip" of discipline-specific constraints, the advocates of cultural studies are (to their shame) replicating the folly of "an older tradition" of "penitents, pilgrims, and flagellants who ascend not to Cultural Studies but to the mount of Contemplation (see *The Faerie Queene*, I.x) and the vision of the deity (see Plato's *Phaedrus* and Augustine's *On Christian Doctrine*)" (103-04). Note once again that Fish remains consistent in his characterization of a united Christian-Platonic tradition that makes no distinction between Plato and Augustine. But note also that what were initially the prototypes of anti-foundationalist self-consuming artifacts (*SCA* 1-43; 374-82) have now come to represent the essentialist tradition of determinate meaning. By drawing the parallel between cultural studies and his caricature of the "essentialist" tradition, Fish is able to threaten its practitioners with the ultimate condemnation of "essentialism," even as he rhetorically invokes the discourse of idolatry:

> Cultural studies, it would seem, has replaced poetry as the replacement for religion; it is the new altar before which those who cast off their infirmities worship. Cultural studies, [Fred] Inglis intones only half-jokingly, "will make you good" [Inglis 229]. (*PC* 105)

Thus Fish argues that the claim to transcendence made by cultural studies simply repeats the earlier attempt to substitute poetry for religion.

Given that he rejects both of these substitutions (by poetry and cultural studies) precisely because of their imitative claim to transcendence, Fish realizes that he has also rejected the two usual justifications for the study of literature. In the last part of the essay he attempts to offer an alternative to these other types of justification which he has refuted. The "old justification" substituted poetry for religion, making critics the "custodians" for "a repository of wisdom good for all problems and all times." The "new justification" gives critics "a role in the forming of new subjectivities capable of forming a counter-disciplinary practice as part of the construction of an 'oppositional public sphere'" (107):

> The old justification won't work because the strong historicism to which many of us have been persuaded rules out a set of texts that float above all historical conditions dispensing wisdom to those fit to receive it. The new justification won't work because the same strong historicism leaves no room for the special and ahistorical brand of reflective consciousness that discourse analysis supposedly engenders. (107-08)

Having dispensed with both the old and the new justification for professional literary interpretation, we come to the *volta* of his argument:

> If literary interpretation will neither preserve the old order nor create a new one, what can it do and why should anyone practice it? I can't tell you in so many words—a general answer to the question is precisely what my argument will not allow—but perhaps I can show you. My vehicle will be a single line from *Paradise Lost.* (108)

Just as in the first chapter, where the line from *Lycidas* was explicated, not to make a point about the poem but to incarnate a set of professional practices, here again Fish offers an interpretive performance the function of which is to embody the irreducible experience of literary explication. Thus the title of his chapter, "Why Literary Criticism is Like Virtue," works in two ways: first to indicate the character of his indictment of the cultural studies claim to "make you good"; but then to reflect also the quality of his own positive argument that literary interpretation, like virtue, is its own inarticulatable reward. Professional practices always already constitute their own self-justified ends. The ends, or *teloi*, of professional practice will always be operative; however, they will always be internal to that discipline. Once again, the core of Fish's argument is that critical self-awareness or "reflection" is either "the extension of a practice and can claim no distance from it [i.e., that practice] or it is itself a [separate] practice and has no privileged relationship to, or even any necessary significance for, practices other than itself" (107). Because no privileged position is available from which to view his own interpretive assumptions, his argument requires that he cannot explicitly state his own practices (much less their justification). Thus, in answering the question as to why anyone should bother practicing literary interpretation in the first place, he must simply *do* literary criticism in the hope that his audience will eventually "catch on" or begin to believe (only because, of course, in a sense, they do already).

It would therefore seem that, if the whole point of the rest of that chapter is to "embody" an interpretive practice, then the choice of which particular "text" to explicate is irrelevant. And yet this is not entirely the case. The earlier allusions to "idolatry" (i.e., cultural studies' lapse into claims of transcendence) now return with full rhetorical force because the line that Fish chooses to analyze from *Paradise Lost* is itself an indictment of idolatry. The line "occurs mid-way in Book 1, just as the narrator is about to call the roll of fallen angels, who, he says, will in future times pass themselves off as gods to credulous mortals" (*PC* 108): "And Devils to adore for Deities" (*PL* 1.373). The direction of Fish's explication is by now familiar: he focuses upon the reader's experience of negotiating between the various ways to interpret the line. Initially, the line seems to show contempt for anyone who would make such a mistake, but then the structure of the line itself seems to suggest a mirroring proximity between devils and deities. The line therefore implies simultaneously that the difference between devils and deities is both small and great. Fish resolves the apparent tension in the line by pointing out that both senses are operative, "but at different levels" (*PC* 109). He then makes his classic contrast between the "carnal" eye that depends upon appearances and the "inner eye"of faith that sees eternal (non-sensible) reality:

> Those who mistake devils for deities do not experience an empirical failure; they experience the failure that is empiricism, the failure to distinguish between the things that are made and the maker, who is, of course, invisible. (109)

God is invisible, just like interpretive assumptions. This is, of course, not only an explication of this particular line from *Paradise Lost,* but also yet another opportunity to draw out a Miltonic/Augustinian analogue for the primacy of interpretive assumptions—complete with citations of Hebrews 11 (*PC* 109). Fish draws out a further analogue by elaborating on the mention of Mammon, a few lines later, where the demon's mistaken focus on the appearance of gems and gold leads him to esteem hell as comparable to heaven (*PL* 1.273; *PC* 109). According to Fish's account, the root problem, for both Mammon and those who fall into idolatry in worshipping demons, is the set of assumptions that give rise to their perceptions. His description of idolatry, as worship misdirected toward the creature rather than the creator, seems entirely commonplace, until we notice that a pivotal element has dropped out of Fish's account, an element that both Milton and Augustine would insist is central to idolatry. Fish reconstrues the notion of idolatry so that the dimension of personal responsibility is completely missing. The broader importance of this shift (which has inhabited his appropriation of both Milton and Augustine all along) will become evident only as we proceed, but clearly Fish has changed something crucial to the usual understanding of idolatry if it now becomes an unavoidable function of interpretive assumptions.

Fish's explicit point in doing the analysis is to demonstrate how, for him, "the reward and pleasure of literary interpretation lie in being able to perform analyses like this" (110). Yet even here the invocations of religious discourse continue, as he describes his admitting to such pleasure as "confession" (110):

> I like uncovering the incredibly dense pyrotechnics of a master artificer, not least because in praising the artifice I can claim a share in it. And when those pleasures have been (temporarily) exhausted, I like linking one moment in a poem to others and then to moments in other works, works by the same author or by his predecessors or contemporaries or successors. It doesn't finally matter which, so long as I can *keep going,* reaping the cognitive and tactile harvest of an activity as self-reflexive as I become when I engage in it. (110; original emphasis)

The "confession" is striking in its juxtaposition of "sins" that cannot possibly committed at the same time. First, he begins speaking as though the author (master artificer) and text had not already been subsumed within the interpretive assumptions of readers. Yet even the latter collectivity is finally reduced to one reader, as the ultimate *telos* for keeping the process going is revealed to be nothing other than the pleasure of self-reflexive diversion. Nevertheless, such a confession does not really qualify as a confession of "sin" (in the sense of something one could be held responsible for, as though one could have done otherwise), because egoism is unavoidable according to Fish (see chap. 3 above). By the end of the passage it becomes clear that the initial impressions of "text" and "author" were mistaken and there was really only one imagination at work all along. The professional critic is now the "master artificer." Fish's confession of egoism continues, however, beyond the linking of the self with the poem:

> Indeed I will take my pleasure wherever I can find it. Thus when I run out of sources and analogues, similarities and differences, I go to the history of criticism which not only allows me to continue the game but to secure my place in it by linking my efforts to those giants of the past. (111)

118

The step from self-absorbed pleasure to active self-promotion is consistent with the logic of the practice as Fish has described it thus far. But the entire pseudo-confession is implicitly absolved by the assumption that such egoism is an unavoidable function of professional practice. In another sense, the rhetoric of confession is appropriate, given that the process of interpretive development that Fish describes, and endorses as his own, directly parallels the classic account of idolatry in the Book of Wisdom. There the process that begins with making statues (interpretive images) to honour "a prince" ends up being an opportunity for "ambitious craftsmen" to glorify themselves by making images that serve only to display their own ingenuity (Wisdom 15:17-21).

But how then does Fish actually deploy the concept of idolatry? It is important, first of all, to point out that his account of false worship has a direct analogue in Augustine's critique of Roman virtue in *The City of God*. Augustine subverts the heroic virtues of Roman culture by analyzing the warrior ethos according to the standards of *caritas*. Ultimately, by redefining justice according to *caritas*, Augustine demonstrates that even the best of Roman virtues are nothing more than vices because they are ultimately rooted in the love of self to the exclusion of God. The virtuous striving necessary to the exercise of Roman virtue, no matter how great, would never be enough to change this fundamental direction of people's collective or individual affections (*CG* 14.7-13, 28; 19.21-28). However, Augustine's point is not that such a change is impossible but that it is effected through repentance, rather than through striving. Fish directly parallels the Augustinian account on this point: his argument for the inefficacy of critical self-awareness (cultural studies' attempts to be "good") runs parallel to the Augustinian critique of Roman virtue. Neither the practice of cultural studies nor the practice of Roman virtue is separable from its central constituting assumptions. However, the difference between Fish's and Augustine's accounts is that Augustine does not allow his account to become a denial of personal or professional responsibility. Fish's consistent manoeuvre is to imply that neither he nor anyone else is responsible for the attitudes that he "confesses" as his credo of professionalism ("I am only enjoying" [*PC* 111]). Naturally, Fish would insist that his implicit denial of responsibility through the depiction of inexorable professional necessity is only a temporary rhetorical gesture within that very process of professional interpretation.

Although he assumes that egoism *per se* is unavoidable, Fish does imply that "idolatry"—in his sense of the term (i.e., the heresy of claiming transcendent or determinate truth)—can be avoided. In fact, he suggests that

119

his own account of professionalism is the only way to avoid such idolatry. In explicating the line, "And Devils to adore for Deities," from *Paradise Lost,* Fish asserts that the "master text" is *Areopagitica* (*PC* 109):

> Good and evill . . . in the field of the World grow up together almost insepara- bly; and the knowledge of good is so involv'd and interwoven with the knowl- edge of evill, and in so many cunning resemblances hardly to be discern'd, that those confused seeds which were imposed on Psyche as an incessant labour to cull out, and sort asunder, were not more intermixed. (*Areopagitica* 514)

Based on this passage, as well as a broader interpretation of both *Paradise Lost* and *Areopagitica,* Fish maintains that Milton's intention is to exhort the reader to an interminable process of interpretation:

> The result is "incessant labour," an interpretive labour, whose yield is not the calculation of the right answer but the experience of how difficult it is "in the field of this World" to determine what the right answer is, how difficult it is to tell the difference between devils and deities. (*PC* 110)

Fish's point here is consistent with his larger analysis of *Areopagitica,* offered in "Driving from the Letter: Truth and Indeterminacy in Milton's *Areopagitica.*" In that essay, Fish argues that Milton viewed any sense of determinate meaning as "idolatry":

> The temptation to idolatry, of surrendering ourselves to the totalizing claims of some ephemeral agenda, can only be resisted by the relentless multipli- cation of that which signifies our lack, the relentless multiplication of dif- ference. ("Driving" 247)

Of course, this account of Milton's position sounds suspiciously like Fish's own indictment of cultural studies (it falls into idolatry by arrest- ing the play of signifiers, or rather, demanding that professional liter- ary interpretation be something other than the means of its own preser- vation). We shall not challenge Fish's reading of Milton here; however, there is one important difference between Fish's own indeterminacy and his reading of Milton's indeterminacy. The possibility of anything being judged as truly "ephemeral" necessarily drops out of Fish's account because importance is constitutionally conferred upon an object as soon as it comes under the purview of (i.e., is constituted by) professional practice. In fact, Milton would likely have viewed precisely such endless deferral as an "ephemeral agenda." Nevertheless, the par- allel between the two accounts is striking. Basically, in order to avoid falling into "idolatry" (determinacy) we need only follow (we cannot avoid following?) Fish's account of "professional correctness," which is the same as Milton's ongoing "interpetive labour."

If we briefly compare Fish's account of idolatry to that given by Augustine, we can see not only how the latter stands apart from the all-subsuming dichotomy of opposing views that Fish refutes, but also how the Augustinian alternative helps to elucidate the ends, or *teloi*, of Fish's position. Once again, Fish's primary objection to cultural studies is that its practitioners have deluded themselves into thinking that they *can* appeal to something transcendent—in this case, subjectivities rather than texts—even as they apparently disclaim such appeals. Fish refutes that position by demonstrating how the valorization of the awareness of contextual constraints is still a tacit appeal to objective (ahistorical) truth (i.e., "idolatry"). The key here is that Fish's argument once again depends upon the subject/object distinction, even as he collapses it in order to refute the efficacy of reflexive self-awareness. As I demonstrated in chapter 5, Augustine does not participate in the aporias resulting from that dichotomy because the process of self-reflection in his account is predicated, not upon the potency of a transcending subject mastering objects in the world, but upon a trust in an inter-personal creator God who is *caritas*. Moreover, the *telos* of that reflection is the same *caritas* who is *veritas* and entails a mode of alterity that is not reducible to the subject/object terms of scientific control. Underlying the call to love God and neighbor is an understanding of the human person as *imago Dei*. The Augustinian critique of idolatry does have a dimension of necessity to it, but it is one of conditional rather than absolute necessity. His point is simply that *if* we do not love and respect God aright (as creator and redeemer, etc.), we will inevitably fail to love God's creatures properly, especially humans who bear the image of God as persons. No matter how much one strives to love other people, that striving will always be inherently selfish without this basic reorientation of the affections toward God. Therefore, idolatry, in Augustinian terms, will manifest itself in the damage that it does to persons, both to the self and others. However, because idolatry is essentially an affection for creatures (even personal ones) that displaces the personal creator, a reorienting of the affections (repentance) remains possible in a way that Fish's quasi-determinism does not allow. For these reasons, an Augustinian critique of literary professionalism would necessarily proceed along neither of the two main lines of objection that Fish addresses in his argument—neither that of the quasi-Platonic conservatives who hypostasize the texts, nor the cultural studies practitioners who objecify critical self-awareness.

Those two main critiques of professional literary practice that Fish addresses—"conservative" and "new historicist"—could be summarized as follows: the former opposes professionalism because of its tendency to be exclusively academic, too narrowly specialized (using arcane jargon); the latter opposes it because of its complicity with the status quo and its failure to effect radical reform in the extra-professional world (42-43). Fish assumes the former position to be already discredited for most of his audience and so he focuses his response on the latter. Each critique is, of course, a respective function of the two usual justifications for the study of literature which Fish has already addressed. However, an Augustinian critique stands apart from both of these, as is evident from the different character of the questions that it asks. The root question that an Augustinian critique would ask regarding professional literary practice today is *not*, "How does the interpetation of these texts broaden our humane understanding of the world?" Nor would it be, "What is the character of the self-knowledge (or institutional transformation) made possible through the reading or writing process?" Although both questions may indeed eventually become part of an Augustian inquiry into the practice, they do not address the core issue. Instead, an assessment in terms of *caritas* would ask, "What are the ends of professional literary practice—that is, what kinds of ultimate affections does it inspire among its practitioners—and what are its effects on persons?" Augustine would, of course, suspect that, insofar as it explicitly refuses to serve any *telos* beyond itself, such professional practice would tend toward idolatry. But what about its treatment of persons?

We have already observed how Fish employs the passages from book 1 of *Paradise Lost*, regarding idolatry and Mammon, to support his argument for the primacy of interpretive assumptions. Mammon is a convenient example for Fish, in helping to reduce idolatry to a matter of blameless "perception" constituted by inaccessible assumptions. However, between the line, "And Devils to adore for Deities," and the description of Mammon, the epic narrator also introduces the character of Moloch. Fish eschews notice of this character, perhaps because, although Moloch's followers do suffer from a perception problem, the account is less susceptible to Fish's emphasis upon predetermined assumptions:

> First *Moloch*, horrid King besmear'd with blood,
> Of human sacrifice, and parents' tears,
> Though for the noise of Drums and Timbrels loud
> Thir children's cries unheard, that pass'd through fire
> To this grim idol. (*PL* 1.392-96)

Human sacrifice is not incidental but central to the worship of Moloch. The parents may love their children more than the "grim idol," but Moloch promises a greater "good" for them than any they could obtain from their children. This is why the parents, despite their tears, sacrifice their children. This is the same logic of unavoidable egoism assumed by Fish's account of professionalism. It may seem distortive to suggest that the logic of professionalism entails anything similar to the human sacrifice of Moloch-worship. But because an Augustinian critique would evaluate professional practice according to its effects upon persons, the analysis would necessarily consider the human consequences. Of course, a study of the children (first-born or otherwise) who are sacrificed in worship to the gods of professional literary practice could violate the disciplinary boundaries between professional literary interpretation and professional sociology. Nevertheless, the nature of a critique based on *caritas* would require that precisely such claims to disciplinary self-containment be challenged. Moreover, because the nature of professionalism more broadly understood (entailing both ever-narrowing focus and ever-increasing production demands) is not separable from the larger machinations of technocratic consumer culture, the image of Moloch is entirely appropriate here. As Paul Ricoeur puts it: "Mythical language is the most faithful way to express power which is without bounds" (117). This is not to say that professionalism is an unbounded evil, but that the dynamics of professionalism are only a local (Western post-industrial) form of service to a transnational technocratic system which presumes its own power to be limitless and its hegemony inexorable—a typical demonic delusion.

Augustine's point would *not* be that a given professional person is forever incapable of *caritas* (as Fish's account of unavoidable egoism implies), but that the system of professional practice tends to ensure that those who are most successful in the system can only be so to the same extent that they become (wittingly or not) embedded in an idolatrous practice whose ultimate end is death (initially of others, but ultimately of the self). The system can be resisted and often is, but never without exacting a price. The logic of professionalism is such that the system which confers identity upon its members then requires those members to make sacrifices in order to guarantee their continued success—this is the logic of Moloch-worship. But surely this is going too far. How could Fish's explication of *Paradise Lost* seriously contribute to the replication of the dynamics of Moloch-worship (i.e., human sacrifice) within professional literary practice? His explication of the passage from the epic is offered as an example of a self-justifying professional

123

practice within an argument which defends that practice as such. In keeping with the self-contained character of that practice, the only ultimate end of its practitioners is their self-interested pleasure and self-promotion (*PC* 110-11). His defense of professional practice (of which the reading of Milton is a part) serves to justify the continued egoism of that practice as being unavoidable. The endorsement of egoism can then be used to justify the choice to sacrifice the lives of others (e.g., students, graduate students, junior colleagues) whenever the professional system offers benefits that are believed to be greater than those that the always-already-selfishly-motivated care for others could ever obtain. Because his argument is predicated on the unavoidability of egoism, the only important point of question within his account is whether professional literary interpretation is the best means by which to achieve that self-serving.

It may be more correct to name as "Moloch," not professionalism itself, but the larger system of technocratic consumer culture of which professional literary interpretation is only one aspect. Yet if that is the case, then professional practice is still a form of Moloch-*worship* (rather than *being* Moloch itself—much like the distinction between *philosophia* and *sophia*). We have already demonstrated how Fish's account of constructivism tends to reinscribe the fact-value distinction, even as he claims to transcend it, because he endorses a position that cannot avoid complicity in the project of technocratic mastery. Fish continues to maintain this position in *Professional Correctness,* as evidenced by his response to a quotation from Terry Eagleton:

> It is no small irony that in making this confession [of professional self-interest] I have come round to the very position Terry Eagleton articulates when he declares "what the aesthetic imitates in its very glorious futility, its pointless self-referentiality, in all its full-blooded formalism, is nothing less than human existence itself, which needs no rationale beyond its own delight, which is an end in itself and which will stoop to no external determination." ([Eagleton 30] *PC* 110)

Fish responds to this would-be indictment:

> I couldn't have said it better, and I also agree with that part of Eagleton's analysis which finds aesthetic pleasure operating both as a support and guarantor of dominant modes of thought and as a challenge to those same modes. But at the moment I am neither supporting nor challenging, but just plain enjoying.
> (*PC* 111)

The last sentence must, of course, be taken as facetiously disingenuous, because his "enjoying" is obviously part of his deeper attempt to "sup-

124

port" the professional enterprise. The need for such support provides the imperative that underlies the main argument that he has been mounting throughout the entire book. And even the intelligibility of his playful comment, "neither supporting nor challenging," requires precisely what his argument has disallowed thus far: the belief in a perception or demonstrative account that exists prior to valuative judgments. It might seem that Fish's playful tone keeps him from really advocating such a return to the fact-value distinction. His response to Eagleton, however, does explicitly endorse (as being inevitable) a "full-blooded formalism" (110; see also 51-52).

It seems that Fish's interpretive quest is now nearing the point of return to its beginning. The journey that began by focusing on the reader's experience in order to escape the inadequacies of formalism has now come full circle and returned to an outright endorsement of formalism. Characteristically, Fish would likely insist that he is not actually endorsing formalism, he is simply pointing out that formal strategies are all that anyone has ever been practicing all along, no matter how much they claimed to be forging alternatives to such aesthetic practices. Nevertheless, precisely such a *reconfigured* formalism demonstrates that Stanley Fish has indeed returned to the place where he began, only to know it for the first time.

CHAPTER SEVEN

Memory

Lest the readers of *Professional Correctness* remain at all uncertain regarding the seriousness with which Fish insists upon the unavoidability of formal interpretive strategies—or whether he has indeed returned to his starting place—his republication of *Surprised by Sin* in 1997 removes all doubt. The lengthy new "Preface to the Second Edition" constitutes an entire additional essay on *Paradise Lost*; however, the main text of *Surprised by Sin* remains identical to the 1967 imprint. Properly speaking, it was in *Surprised by Sin* (subtitled "The Reader in *Paradise Lost*") that Fish first made extensive use of what has become his trademark approach of giving detailed attention to the reader's experience of the interpretive process. In this respect, his analysis might be described more accurately as "phenomenological" rather than as technically "formalist." Indeed, *Surprised by Sin* effectively marks the beginning of Fish's movement into "reader-response" criticism. However, at that point (1967) in the development of his thinking (even before *Self-Consuming Artifacts*), he treated not only readerly subjectivity but also textual structures and authorial intentions as objectively stable entities.[1] For example, in describing the treatment of God the Father in *Paradise Lost*, Fish does not hesitate to assert that "Milton constructs his narrative in such a way as to make the avoidance of response, and therefore choice . . . , impossible [for the reader]" (*SS* 90). Only later does Fish come to abandon each of these (author, textual structure, and reader) in favor of an all-embracing interpretive process that constitutes each element and is the engine of its own transformation. And yet, the implications of precisely those arguments over the intervening thirty years, the arguments that progressively describe that reading process in greater detail, are ultimately so all-encompassing that they leave the initial terms of formalist discourse quite literally unchanged—thus the 1967 and 1997 imprints of the main text of *Surprised by Sin* are identical. Given our account of the developments in Fish's position so far, we already have some sense of how this came about. As we now bring Fish's concept of faith into a concluding direct engagement with that of Augustine, the event of republication offers a fitting occasion for our closing reflections on the continuities within Fish's quest.

Because there will always already be disciplinary constraints regarding, for example, the use of some (though not all) terms, or where to look for evidence and so forth, Fish can employ the terms like "author," "structure," and "reader" without qualification (even in the 1997 Preface). He can do so because it seems that the use of these terms can now be understood (within professional literary interpretation at least) not necessarily to imply a belief in Enlightenment subjectivity. Yet a deeper consistency between the new Preface and the old arguments of the main text also raises questions about the theoretical/anti-theoretical claims that he developed in the time between them:

> You will probably have noticed that in the course of defending *Surprised by Sin,* I have repeated the gesture that most infuriated some of its readers. I have turned objectors into devils and replied to their points by hitting them over the head with mine. . . . The circularity of this is obvious but it is not one for which I apologize since circularity, of a deep not meretricious kind, is what I attribute to Milton's universe where . . . all virtues are one virtue—acknowledgement of and obedience to God—and all errors one error—falling away from the worship of God to the worship of secondary forms. Literary criticism does not stand outside this vast circularity and it should be no surprise that my judgement on what critics say is inseparable from, and follows predictably from my judgement of what Milton is (always) saying.
>
> (*SS*, Preface lxv-lxvi)

Despite the admission of circularity with respect to Milton criticism, this passage also demonstrates that Fish's arguments in the intervening thirty years have always involved a conflation of "what Milton is saying" with his own theoretical claims about the primacy of interpretive assumptions, or "belief." The last sentence in the above passage is a classic instance of the pivotal shift that Fish has made throughout his theoretical arguments by tacitly collapsing what he describes as Milton's position into his own. The moment at which he transfers the "vast circularity" of "Milton's universe" onto literary criticism in general, Fish is applying the dynamics of Milton's universe to the universe at large, and presuming to adopt Milton's position as his own. Of course, Fish is careful to qualify his position as being a specific claim about Milton's authorial intention (albeit problematized); but it is by now clear that Fish's account of reading Milton's poetry is an antecedent for his account of all reading. Nor are we surprised when Fish later connects Milton's view of politics and human history with Augustine's rule of charity (liii). The numerous analogues between the passage just cited and Fish's various evolving arguments for the primacy of interpretive assumptions should by now be transparent; however, the silent way that Fish secularizes "Milton's universe" is also directly parallel to his treatment of Augustine. In one sense, such secularization is simply a matter of course, given the present character of the interpretive community of Milton scholars (as Fish would point out), but what Fish never considers is whether the "deep not meretricious" circularity of Milton's universe can remain so when denied its central theological truth claim. How does the admitted circularity of Fish's own rigorously secular account then avoid becoming meretricious?

At the outset of this investigation we raised the question of whether readers can "choose" their interpretive assumptions. The question itself requires certain assumptions about the possibility and efficacy of choice in relation to consciously perceived options. Both Fish and Augustine reject the idea of the autonomous rational subject whose decisions are completely unconstrained or who is able to hold before itself all possible belief options. However, Fish's account depends upon a conflation of three different senses of belief or "faith": (1) conscious assumptions; (2) unconscious assumptions; (3) a belief in the primacy of (2), often elided with (1), in shaping all thought processes. The key difference is that Augustine's account maintains that the insight into the primacy of belief is inextricable from an apprehension of what the substantive content of conscious faith should be. By failing to articulate any correlative sense of faith content in his analysis, Fish's account reinscribes the myth of the autonomous liberal subject; for that is the only story according to which *what* you believe is not nearly so important as *that* you believe something. This is why Fish's vacuous "faith in faith" *does* ultimately find content in professionalism. The gods of agnosis are finally revealed to be the underlings of technocratic mastery: Moloch's servants. We can see the character and the depth of the connection between Fish's position and the dynamics of technological control by looking more closely at the dyadic "conscious" versus "unconscious" opposition which enables his different senses of the term "faith."

Fish rightly insists that constructivism *per se* has no consequences, and thus demonstrates that the circularity of his account provides no guidance in helping one to decide which conscious set of interpretive assumptions to employ; however, that point also allows an implicit disclaimer of responsibility (corporate or individual) for the real human consequences resulting from the practice of professional literary interpretation. Fish rejects the formalist claim to objectivity, but he retains the formalist pretense to avoid all extra-disciplinary value claims. He would likely respond to such concerns by insisting that he is not advocating an abdication of responsibility or denying that people do hold one another accountable, but rather that they will always do so within a context where certain assumptions (not necessarily the same ones across time or space) will dictate what constitutes responsible behavior, etc. The problem with such a position is that, in spite of whatever Fish might claim about its strict "inapplicability," such a generalization is evidently most useful for evading or dismissing specific charges of irresponsibility when they arise.

There is, however, a deeper issue that needs to be addressed: to admit such a constructivist generalization about responsibilities encourages a blindness to the needs of others who are not members of a given community (professional or otherwise). This aspect of the problem becomes especially apparent at the very end of *Professional Correctness,* where Fish, given the self-contained nature of any justification for professional literary interpretation, attempts to address the question of how to justify the academic literary enterprise to the public—that is, to those outside the professional community, those often providing the money. His ultimate response is that because we have little reason to hope that the current generation of university presidents will anytime soon reclaim their positions as public intellectuals, English departments need to "hire lobbyists":

> I don't mean the damage-control types found in most university public relations offices, who are even more timid than their bosses. . . . No I mean publicity-seeking types who are always thinking of ways to grab huge hunks of newspaper space or air time and fill it with celebrations of the university so compelling that millions of Americans will go to bed thankful that the members of the Duke English Department are assuring the survival and improvement of Western civilization. (*PC* 126)

Ironic or not, this statement demonstrates explicitly that the primary consequence of "professional correctness," as Fish describes it, is to ensure the financial security and advancement solely of those practicing the profession without the slightest attention to the genuine needs of those whom the profession ostensibly serves, or at least formerly claimed to serve: students. Naturally, Fish would respond to such concerns by pointing out that he is not ignoring the needs of students but is, rather, advocating the use of "publicity-seeking" professionals in order to secure the financial support that will enable continued service to students. But according to Fish's account, the only thing that professional literary interpretation can offer students is the opportunity for a select few of them to become professional beneficiaries of a system that is supported by the public and the majority of paying students who are unable themselves to become professional aesthetes. Thus, even though Fish would insist that his position does not require a denial of responsibility for the consequences of professional practices, the practical consequences of his argument involve precisely the kind of incapacity to allow for alterity that such a denial entails.

There is also a further sense in which the core of Fish's repeated central argument justifies a denial of individual responsibility. Throughout his analyses, he implies that the immediate inaccessibility of those assumptions which enable understanding entails absolution of any culpability for the actions dictated by those unconscious beliefs. When he makes the point that "one doesn't 'choose' one's readings" (*PC* 48), Fish draws upon a sense of the word "choice" that is linked exclusively with the Enlightenment vision of unconstrained subjectivity so that he can already dismiss it as untenable. Indeed, presumably no plausible model of freedom (pre- or postmodern) advocates such a view, but he implies that the only alternative to it is either radical determinism or his own moderate position (modelled, of course, on Milton and Augustine). Yet Fish's own account cannot avoid implying certain conclusions about the interaction between understanding and volition. To draw out those implications in relation to Augustine's position is to see how Fish's central equation of consciousness with knowledge leads his argument to a pivotal incoherence.

Augustine's account of human knowing and immediate volition includes not only consciousness, but also memory and affections. Augustine's emphasis upon affections is based upon the apprehension that our moment-by-moment choices are dictated by what we love most, often despite conscious efforts to act differently. Such efforts will always be of negligible efficacy until we reorient our root affections. This is why Fish concurs with Augustine in pointing out that reflexive self-awareness has no efficacy in itself; the source of our immediate choice at that moment remains inaccessible to us. However, Fish makes two further deductions that do not follow from an actual Augustinian position and are indeed refuted by a fuller account of *caritas*. First, Fish construes that limitation upon immediate consciousness in quasi-deterministic terms, implicitly (and selectively) allowing the element of human responsibility to drop from consideration, whereas Augustine's point would be that we need to change the ultimate object of our affections (i.e., repent). Second, Augustine would insist that reflexive self-awareness can have some efficacy, but only if the *telos* of that reflection is *caritas*, rather than the rational mastery of objects in the world. The version of reflexive self-awareness that Fish rejects is precisely the rationalist approach which defines reality in terms of objects apprehended by an assumed ego, toward which all knowing is directed. Because Augustinian reflection begins and ends with the creaturely apprehension of the *caritas* who is *veritas*, such self-awareness is neither predicated on a privileging of "objectivity," nor does it participate in the illusory attempt to valorize the awareness of the impossibility of objectivity. Reflection oriented toward *caritas*, rather than rationalist mastery, does not claim to be free from contextual constraints, but attempts instead to set the affections fully toward Christ and thereby to preserve an openness to the alterity of creatures (human and non-human) and their works. Thus reflexive self-awareness can be effective, within the Augustinian account, insofar as it enables repentance, the origin and end of which, when combined with faith in Christ, is the love of God and neighbor.

The crucial question then is not, "How should/can I choose my interpretive assumptions?" but rather, "Whom do I love, as revealed by the *telos* of my life's actions?" The answer to that question will indicate who ultimately will be served by my interpretive activity, professional or otherwise. Whether we consciously choose the ends of our interpretive practices or not, our root affections will be served. Once again, the fact that we are not immediately conscious of whom we serve, or sacrifice, by our interpretive activity does not preclude our responsibility, because self-reflection, though never context-free or entirely objective, can show us something of the basic orientation of our affections. There is, admittedly, some opacity in the Augustinian account (in *Confessions* for example) regarding precisely how grace enables people not merely to apprehend the orientation of their affections but also to turn them around—that is to turn from self-love to love of God and neighbor, rather than simply to admit the unavoidability of egoism. Nevertheless, notwithstanding the obscurity of the operations of grace, we are still responsible (omniscience is not a prerequisite for moral accountability)—we can accept or refuse grace. Here we come to the root of the difference between the two characterizations of human finitude and freedom. Both Augustine and Fish insist upon the radically limited nature of human understanding, but there is a world of difference between recognizing that, as finite creatures, we can either accept or reject the grace that we need, and insisting that there is no grace. The irony here is that in *Is There a Text?* Fish sarcastically suggests that the doctrine of original sin (an inherited perversity of the will) is the "only relevant model" for those who believe in "determinate" textual meaning to account for differences in interpretive results (*ITTC* 338).[2] Now as Fish finds himself explicitly advocating a "full-blooded formalism" (*PC* 110-11), his own position ends up becoming basically a secularized version of that doctrine— that is, the inexorable bondage of the will, except without the possibility of "salvation" (the only escape is to leave the given profession or the entirety of academe, which is to cease existing "professionally").

At a slightly different level of consideration, it should now be apparent that Fish's repeated construction of the interpretive process so as to avoid any ascription of responsibility is, in effect, an attempt to side-step the entire issue of the human will. However, that avoidance is in itself evidence of some felt need to absolve oneself—evidence that people do inevitably hold one another responsible for certain choices, regardless of whether or not we formulate an explicit belief in a "volitional faculty" as such. The question of responsibility leads us to consider how Fish's avoidance reconfigures the Augustinian account of the relation between the memory, will and understanding. What drops out of Fish's account is the crucial difference between choosing actions whose consequences we do not "know" (that is, we are not capable of considering the consequences at any time up to the present) and choosing actions the consequences of which we are not immediately conscious (though we "know" the consequences, in the sense that we could consider them if we chose to do so at a given moment).

The Augustinian category of memory offers a crucial distinction which has far-reaching consequences, a distinction which is lost in Fish's account. At the most basic level, the Augustinian sense of "memory" consists of those things which we *could* bring to our present attention but do not, in the everyday sense that we all "know" things of which we are not immediately conscious. As is evident from the entire process of personal recollection in *Confessions*, "memory" for Augustine includes our experience of sense perception and imagination (not simply innate ideas), and so it cannot be equated with the Platonic or Pythagorean concept of memory (*Conf.* 10.8). At the same time, the open admission of memory's severe limitations and gaps (10.8-9) demonstrates that Augustine is not appealing to it as a category of complete or infallible knowledge. The ultimate value of consulting the partial and fallible memory is not to provide determinate propositions from which to build certainty but to discern the overall trajectory of one's affections. Such a discernment does not even entail an enumeration of our moment-by-moment volitional actions in their totality (a

132

genuinely impossible self-reflective task), but rather an apprehension of the will's orientation. Moreover, the human capacity to render conscious experience intelligible depends upon an act of the will in relation to memory and understanding—that is, their indivisible triunity (*Trin.* 14.8; 10.11.18). The act of remembering is a conscious act, but the faculty of memory includes precisely those things of which we are not immediately conscious. Why is this important? The fact that we cease to think about something consciously does not mean that we cease to know it. This might seem like an extraordinarily banal observation, except that precisely such a distinction is what Fish's account of interpretive assumptions no longer allows. If we recall Fish's basic characterization of interpretive assumptions—always simultaneously unavoidable yet inaccessible—we may be struck by its apparent similarity to Augustinian memory. In one sense it is true that both interpretive assumptions and *memoria* involve an immediately unconscious principle that enables conscious intellection. However, the similarity is misleading, because the Augustinian model allows for a distinction between knowledge and consciousness.[3]

Because his account elides any distinction between knowing something and being immediately aware of it—such that to state that we are "aware" of our biases means that we "know" they exist—Fish implies that if we are not immediately aware of the consequences of a given action at the moment of choice, then we do not "know" what the consequences would be. In effect, we should not hold ourselves responsible for actions whose consequences we know (in the sense that we *could* have made ourselves conscious of them) to be harmful or even devastating to others if we are not immediately conscious of those consequences. This demonstrates that despite his apparent emphasis upon the temporal sequence of the reading process, Fish's account revealingly ends up denying altogether the obviously temporal character of human consciousness. In Augustine's account, those actions which a person chooses may feel inexorable, and be experienced as such because the person has *already* chosen the goal, the *telos*, toward which that action moves the self. We may not be immediately conscious that we are choosing a given action, because the decision is dictated by affections that were formed long ago and may have been further shaped by habit; nevertheless, we are still responsible for such choices because we are responsible to examine and "know" (i.e., not necessarily be continually *aware* of) the direction of our affections. In effect, for Augustine, people who never stop long enough to reflect on their own lives will never repent, because repentance presumes a certain minimal degree of self-knowledge, and ultimately entails discerning the *telos* of our root affections. Moreover, this reorientation of the affections results in actions that have consequences not just personally, but professionally as well.

The broader issue of understanding thus turns on the distinction between historically reflective self-knowledge and immediately conscious self-awareness, a distinction that Fish denies by equating "critical self-awareness" with all self-knowledge. Thus self-reflection, in Fish's account, has no efficacy because it can never provide the freedom from contextual constraints that the assumed objectivist paradigm requires. In contrast, the Augustinian conception of memory (which is not detachable from an admittedly fallible apprehension of the notion of personhood rooted in the Trinity) entails that self-knowledge is distinct from immediate self-consciousness and is never claimed as "objective." Consequently, self-reflection can, according to Augustine, be effective, not in providing knowledge for mastering objects, but in allowing a reorientation of the affections toward the *veritas* of the triune God who subsists in the relation of *caritas*.

But what are the implications of all this for Fish's account of reading strategies? Once again it reveals the deeply textualist, even Ramist, imperatives that inform his project. As we established in chapter 4, it was precisely the consideration of *memoria* that dropped from Ramist rhetorical training, because Ramist dialectical method was based on the elaborate visual-textual structure of bifurcating tables "designed to implement recall" (Ong, Introduction 157). Once again, this arbitrary division of rhetoric from memory, like the division between rhetoric and dialectic, was based on "pedagogical convenience rather than on any profound insight into the nature of thought and expression" (159). It may seem strange to link Fish's position with the reductively spatial thinking of Peter Ramus, and yet there is a direct correspondence between them in the complete removal of memory from the generally assumed account of discursive practice upon which Fish draws. Because he does not allow for the integral role of memory in rhetoric, or human knowing in general, Fish is then able implicitly to equate immediate consciousness with the "will," in the sense of the seat of moral responsibility. This is ultimately what permits the disclaimer of culpability for any action, professional or otherwise, that is not a function of immediately conscious choices. With the loss of memory as a category, so too the historical dimension of consciousness is lost. The continuous operation of unconscious assumptions ensures the ongoing (but selective) availability of claims to blameless "ignorance" (assuming that "knowing" means "immediately conscious of"). Thus Fish can imply throughout his account of "professional correctness" that he is both unsurprised by the unavoidable egoism of professional practice—unsurprised by sin—and yet also able to presume that such "sin" can be dismissed as a blameless function of unconscious interpretive assumptions.

Moreover, the deletion of the category of memory from Fish's account of human knowing informs not only his most recent defense of professional practice, but also the account of reading assumed by the main critical argument of *Surprised by Sin*. The central, and commonly noted, difficulty in that argument might be called "the problem of the eternally naive reader." The analysis of *Paradise Lost* brings to bear substantial background erudition and textual sensitivity, but also simultaneously requires the paradoxical implication that such a reading experience is always the first (hence the "surprise"). What drops out of Fish's implied account of the reading experience is, again, and still, memory. The failure to make a distinction between the first and second reading of a poem is precisely where other reader-response critics like Hans Robert Jauss and Wolfgang Iser would see the entire argument of *Surprised by Sin* as deeply flawed. Both Jauss and Iser point out that what makes a second reading (and all those after) of an imaginative work so crucially different from a first is that only during the second attempt is our moment-by-moment reading able to relate each part of the experience to a particularized sense of the whole work, rather than a purely anticipatory sense of the whole based only on generic considerations, etc. (cf. Jauss 25-28; Iser 280-81). Fish is certainly correct to emphasize the generally educative process involved in reading *Paradise Lost*. But if we admit that the epic was expected to be read more than once by a given reader, then we must allow for the role of memory in all subsequent readings, such that both the character and content of that "education" are different from that entailed for Fish's perpetually naive reader. Moreover, my point here is not to be confused with the objection raised by Bill Readings (addressed in the new Preface to *Surprised by Sin*) that Fish's account involves a "desperate striving for the reconstruction of the act of first reading" (*SS* xiv). Fish responds to such criticism by gladly admitting that he is "producing" a new experience rather than claiming to "recover" an originary one (xiv). The point being made here is that even in the logic of his claim to "produce" a new experience (thereby arguing that the poem confronts the reader with a series of "interpretive crises" [xiv]), Fish's production proceeds as if the reader were always naive (without memory of a previous reading experience of the whole poem).

On the other hand, the root of Fish's charge against the likes of Jauss and Iser (and their predecessor Gadamer) is that they continue to

135

believe in the efficacy of reflexive self-awareness—a belief that Fish (as we have seen) rejects as contradictory because it claims that one can be both historically conditioned yet also able to escape history somehow (e.g., *DWCN* 68-86 on Iser; cf. *PC* 129). The effectiveness of both Fish's and his opponents' critiques requires that, in order for an account of the reading process to avoid either falling into solipsism or making tacit claims to ahistorical objectivism, we must (unlike Fish) allow for the integral role of memory in reading but also (unlike the Konstanz theorists) allow more consistently for the limitations of historically effected consciousness. Only in the Augustinian apprehension of *caritas* do we find an account of personal and textual alterity that addresses both critiques. It offers an account of memory as integral to the process of understanding (textual or otherwise) that does not end up equating awareness with knowledge; yet it also allows for an efficacious dynamic of self-reflection that does not entail a claim to complete objectivity because its goal is creaturely *caritas* rather than scientific mastery.

Because there is therefore a sense in which neither the second-time reader of *Paradise Lost*, nor Fish's professionally correct literary critic is "surprised by sin," we might ask whether there really is any alternative to "unavoidable egoism." How could a committed rhetorician ever come to the point of facing personal sin? The answer to such a question is writ large in *Confessions* where we find the story of how, in effect, Augustine the rhetorician came to repentance after self-examination— a rhetoric that includes memory. We see the same process "writ small" in book 8 of *Confessions*, where Augustine tells the story of Victorinus the rhetorician. In the story of Victorinus, however, the emphasis is less upon the self-examination leading to repentance and more on the nature of true belief or "faith" (reminding readers that the call to Christ is twofold: repentance *and* belief in Christ). Victorinus was a man of "great learning, with a profound knowledge of all the liberal sciences":

> He had studied a great many books of philosophy and published criticisms of them. He had been master to many distinguished members of the Senate, and to mark his outstanding ability as a teacher, he had even been awarded a statue in the Roman forum—a great honour in the eyes of the world. (8.2)

Well into his old age Victorinus continued to defend "with all the fire of his oratory" the pagan practices "then in vogue amongst most of the nobility of Rome" (8.2). However, after a careful study of the Scriptures and "all Christian literature," Victorinus came to the point where he apparently no longer believed in the gods of Rome and claimed in private to be a Christian:

136

> Privately, as between friends, though never in public, he used to say to Simplicianus, "I want you to know that I am a Christian." Simplicianus used to reply, "I shall not believe it or count you as a Christian until I see you in the Church of Christ." At this Victorinus would laugh and say, "Is it then the walls of the church that make the Christian?" (8.2)

But the reason for Victorinus' refusal to identify publicly with the believing community was not really his theological concern about the spiritual nature of the Church, but rather a fear "of offending his proud friends," knowing that a "storm of hostility would break upon him from the peak of their Babylonian dignity" (8.2). Of course, he would have to face not only the wrath of his friends but also the humiliation, for a public intellectual, of associating with such a socially and intellectually mixed group. At last Victorinus did publicly identify with the Church, but only at that very moment when, in the act of baptism, he personally identified with Christ. The experience of Victorinus shows that the nature of Christian faith is never purely private or individual, but always has public (even professional) consequences as well as personal ones. The step of faith required for Victorinus was precisely one in which he publicly identified with the believing community and then faced the professional as well as personal consequences. His earlier attempt to believe the message without identifying with the community also kept him from identifying personally with Christ in baptism. A living experience of the text and the community could not be separated or collapsed into one another. This leads us back to the point that we established in chapter 3 regarding the dynamic and fruitful tension between the integrity of the believing (interpretive) community and the integrity of the message borne by the text. Thus in order for a rhetorician like Victorinus to have anything more than a vacuous "faith in faith" that rigorously entails no consequences, he must not only engage in the self-examining remembrance that leads to repentance, but must also, in an act of personal trust, publicly identify with the community of faith and believe the content of its claims regarding the person of Christ.

Both Victorinus and Fish see the deeper connections between profession and confession, but they run the implications of that connection in opposite directions. Victorinus discerns that public profession of faith is not finally separable from private confession of belief; whereas Fish uses the rhetoric of confession to defend professional practices because he sees both actions as inherently rhetorical, or simply performative. What remains to be seen is whether Fish is justified in assuming the biconditional equivalence between the two terms that enables his reversal of their usual relation. The tension that Fish exploits is inherent in what has traditionally been understood as the problem of duplicity or hypocrisy. From the possibility of a purely rhetorical profession Fish's account presumes the impossibility of a genuine personal confession. But the possibility of hypocrisy does not dictate its necessity. Moreover, as we found earlier, it is precisely Fish's equation of "faith" with all manner of "inaccessible assumptions" that renders unintelligible the distinction between sincerity and insincerity (see 34-35 above on *DWCN* ix), without which hypocrisy is also unintelligible. As Augustine points out in *City of God,* the precise membership of the true Church is hidden within time (20.7), but that does not disprove the sincerity of public professions of faith made by those for whom such claims are also a personal confession of belief. The crucial point of distinction between the two rhetoricians is that Fish's position obscures his underlying insistence upon the impossibility of ascertaining (for either profession or confession) what the content of conscious faith could or should be—all the while admitting that it must be something. In doing so, the *de facto* content of Fish's faith is finally revealed to be the technocratic primacy of "function": the systematic ordering of all imperatives according to the pretense that the dictates of that ordering are always already in place.[4] As demonstrated by both the (anti)theory and practice of Fish's arguments, the attempt to apprehend the relation between confession and profession as a rhetorical function, rather than as constituted by *caritas,* results in denying the alterity of both texts and persons. Both the confession and profession become constitutionally vacuous, as all otherness is subsumed within the imploding node of a would-be subjectivity on a socio-linguistic matrix.

Because the root of the difficulty in Fish's position lies in his attempt to conceive of "belief" apart from any content, we can now see further why my introductory question—to the effect, "Can we choose our interpretive assumptions? (And if so, How?)"—is so deeply mistaken. Not only does it participate in the aporias of rationalist self-reflection, the kind of reflection that can never be efficacious on its own terms, but as a question it assumes the context of a search for an abstractable interpretive model that can be applied regardless of the particular text in question (i.e., a form independent of content). Even though the question seems to allow that the model could vary according to the content of textual particularities, the very articulation of the question requires that interpretive practices in themselves (as contentless forms or functions) are constitutionally independent and hence separable from any particular content. In contrast, Augustinian *caritas* (as an interpretive *telos*) is never pure form. In one sense, the basic content of *caritas* is presented in the Gospel narratives and summarized in the Apostles' Creed. Yet a genuine apprehension of *caritas* involves not only an understanding of those narrative events, but also a personal and conscious choice to accord oneself to the truth claims of that narrative. After the point of decision, both the content of the narrative understood and the choice of belief in that testimony then become part of the memory from which conscious and unconscious implications follow, resulting ultimately (though not immediately) in the transformation of the whole person. The root issue is one of overall personal direction rather than immediate consciousness, although the two are obviously related in complex ways.

Thus *caritas* is incarnated in the present life of believers collectively and individually, as they seek to be faithful to the truth revealed through the narrative within which they live.[5] But how is this account of the content of Christian faith important to understanding Fish's deployment of faith? It demonstrates that the narrative content of the faith concerning Christ's life, death and resurrection cannot be intelligibly separated from the ethical praxis of that faith. It is precisely that separation between faith-content and faith-action that has inhabited Fish's account of interpretive practice since the early 1960's, when he first adopted as his own "faith" the imperative to negotiate between the "Scylla" of presumptuous interpretive pride and the "Charybdis" of immobile despair (*NSFS* 293; *SCA* 40). Fish must base his ethical imperative upon contentless "faith in faith," in order to conceal the way in which his argument (including his description of a smooth-running professional community) depends upon a residually Christian ethos. This is not to suggest that such virtues as humility and hope (the respective opposites of pride and despair) are exclusively dependent upon Christian faith-content, although many cultures do not insist upon such virtues. Rather, the key point here is that Fish attempts to link those virtues specifically with a faith that has no content whatsoever.[6] He affirms the unavoidablility of faith in something, but he rigorously eschews the admission of conscious trust in anyone or anything in particular. The Augustinian apprehension of *caritas* is predicated upon the insistence that neither the faith-content nor the faith-action can be separated because the *way* that we live ultimately (though not always immediately) reveals *what* we really believe. In this way our actions can show us where self-examination is presently most necessary: for example, what do my actions reveal about my ultimate affections in comparison to what I claim them to be? The central error that runs throughout Fish's argument is the assertion that a contentless "faith in faith" (whether formalist or phenomenological) can sustain the assumed ethical imperatives for humility or hope.

139

We can now begin to see the real consequences—logical, professional and personal—of using theological discourse to defend or explain literary practice in such a way that assumes the ostensible content of the theological terms to be irrelevant. There are indeed few rhetorical moves more common within literary circles (both past and present) than the attempt to appropriate theological discourse to articulate literary arguments. By bringing Fish's deployment of the discourse of "faith" into more direct engagement with the Augustinian account of faith, we have begun to see more clearly some of the implications of Fish's rhetoric. However, an Augustinian critique of literary professionalism—a critique based on *caritas*—does *not* imply the subsuming of literary studies within theology; rather, it insists upon the temporally limited claims of both discourses, upon their right respective relations to an end beyond them both. There is thus a kind of "secularism" that follows from an Augustinian critique of professional literary interpretation.[7] However, there is a vast difference between what might be called the "secular Augustinianism" of someone, for example, like Hannah Arendt, and a theologically based "Augustinian secularism." While the former generally attempts to deploy Augustinian philosophy in the service of thinking about present concerns, it does so while trying to hold in suspension the question of whether God even exists, which in practice amounts to the imperative to think and act *as if* there were no God. Such an approach opposes the most basic Augustinian imperative of *fides quaerens intellectum*. In contrast, a genuinely Augustinian secularism (specifically because it begins in *fides* and ends in *caritas*) insists that a properly ordered literary practice recognizes its limitations and does not make misleading claims (even by allusive linguisitic appropriation) to being an adequate substitute for theological claims. This may sound very similar to Fish's account of Milton's critique of interpretive idolatry: that is, not to ascribe eternal status to our present partial understanding. Indeed, Milton is following Augustinian tradition in that respect. The crucial difference is that Fish is at precisely that moment using Milton's genuinely theological position to defend a literary argument that claims independence from all reality (discursive or otherwise) beyond itself—that is, Fish, in the very act of drawing the analogy between his position and theirs, is doing precisely what Milton and Augustine both argue against.

In closing, it should be noted that Fish is not alone in using theological discourse in a manner that obscures the implications of such appropriation. The same tensions inhabit much of poststructuralist thought in general. On the one hand, theological terminology is rhetorically adopted to defend a given position; on the other, there is either a continuously assumed or briefly mentioned dismissal of the substantive content of such theology on the grounds of its being identified with the illusory Enlightenment prejudice against all prejudice. At the root of this widely shared mischaracterization of much theological content is the belief that "perspectival thinking" somehow subverts the imperatives of all reflective Christian discourse in the same way that it subverts Enlightenment thinking in general. In fact, from Augustine to Nicholas of Cusa, there is absolutely nothing scandalous, or even remotely surprising, about the idea of perspectival thinking in itself (*pace* Nietzsche). Such thinking is scandalous only to those of the Enlightenment dream who have abandoned the premise of creaturely finitude and deceived themselves into thinking that they could occupy a divine perspective.

In order to demonstrate how these mistaken assumptions operate, here is an almost randomly chosen passage from Hans Robert Jauss. In describing the illusions of objectivist historiography, Jauss cites Leopold von Ranke as an example:

> Ranke's famous utterance of 1854 gives a theological foundation to this postulate [of complete historical objectivity]: "But I maintain that each period is immediate vis-à-vis God, and that its value depends not at all on what followed from it, but rather on its own existence, on its own self." (Jauss 7)

The correct term to describe such an Enlightenment account of a historical method that attempts to occupy a "God's-eye-view" is precisely not "theological," as Jauss would have it, but "hubristic" (to the extent of implying that humans can replace, or have replaced, God). When making ostensibly historical claims, such as those in *Self-Consuming Artifacts* or the new Preface to *Surprised by Sin*, Fish accurately establishes, through his deployment of both Augustinian and Miltonic "faith," how genuinely Christian thinking exposes the folly of such Enlightenment hubris. However, when mounting his own theoretical arguments in any of the intervening works, the success of Fish's claims depends upon taking a view like Jauss's which effectively subsumes all theism within modern rationalist metaphysics. To return to the Jauss example above, the ease with which such references to "God"—even when describing capacities being claimed by humans—are taken to be representative of some vaguely "Christian" theological position only indicates the depth at which this mischaracterization of theological traditions still operates as an antecedent for poststructuralist claims to humility. Of course, integral to the plot (*mythos*) of the poststructuralist

141

metanarrative is the notion that perspectival thinking is inherently atheistic. Now that we have established the possibility of perspectival thinking rooted in *caritas*, and with it a less reductive account of alterity, we can begin to discern how misleading this widely assumed story is and to bring it into question. Admittedly, one question which remains, because it can be answered best by readers of this text other than myself, is whether I have been truly charitable in my reading of Stanley Fish. I hope and trust that I have.

NOTES

CHAPTER TWO

[1] Fish's "double argument" (that there is no objective truth but that relativism is also not livable), consistently poses the greatest difficulty for his critics. Fish maintains that while all perceptions of objectivity are constructed, genuine relativism is impossible because everyone is located within an interpretive community or social context (that is, no one is an a-contextual monad). Thus he argues that we cannot hold our own beliefs as though they were anything other than objectively true (*DWCN* 467; *ITTC* 361). Similarly, there are no true "relativists," because people cannot actually live as though their own beliefs were radically in doubt (*ITTC* 360-61). Many of the objections commonly raised against Fish's arguments depend upon forgetting one side or the other of this tension. Even Christopher Norris, one of Fish's most unrelenting (and usually consistent) critics, sometimes adopts this approach against Fish's anti-objectivism. At one point Norris calls Fish's position "ultra-relativist," on the grounds that it encourages acquiescence to the political status quo (Norris, *Uncritical Theory* 127). Elsewhere, Norris's analysis of Fish's position is more rigorous, but here at least, Norris seems to forget that Fish's general position does not argue for or against political oppositional strategies, but points out that there are always even more basic shared assumptions upon which all opposition must depend. Although this kind of problem is an exception for Norris, it is often the norm for other critical treatments of Fish. For example, in the arguments of Carol Barash, Gregory Currie, Oscar Kenshur and James Carney, each at some point raises an objection which depends upon momentarily denying one side of this tension that Fish maintains. Barash ends up arguing that legal practice "*should* be principled" (192; her emphasis), but in doing so reveals that she has missed Fish's insistence that it can never avoid being principled (constrained) in some way. Currie's objections regarding conflicting interpretations and the tensions between "free will" and constraints (214-15) overlook Fish's point that consciousness is constituted by interpretive constraints and that conflicts arise from these inaccessible assumptions. Kenshur suggests that Fish has created a problem for himself by making the critic a creation of the interpretive community (381), but Kenshur forgets that according to Fish all the conscious beings which compose the community are constituted by interpretive assumptions. Carney seems to think that he is refuting Fish by arguing for the unrelenting necessity of some interpretive "decidability" (10), but he simply misses Fish's point, that even the most open-ended interpretive strategy cannot avoid dependence upon some constitutive constraint (decidability).

[2] Aside from the theoretical or anti-theoretical arguments raised later, there are some more practical difficulties that emerge from Fish's double assertion of "anti-objectivism without relativism." Fish insists that his argument does not lead to solipsism, because everyone is part of some interpretive community. However, his argument against the possibility of relativism requires that those beliefs which are necessarily derived from an interpretive community can somehow be lived out in a solipsistic vacuum. Fish's argument ignores the way in which "anti-foundationalist theory hope" operates as a social phenomenon. In his view, people "mistaken-

143

ly" call themselves "relativists" when really they only hold (as objectively true) a set of values different from others around them. However, by simply defining "relativism" out of existence, instead of asking what people who call themselves relativists might actually believe and do, Fish's argument revealingly overlooks the role of the interpretive community. In popular terms, the most basic assumptions of people who call themselves "relativists" usually involve phrases like, "Don't impose your values on other people." Fish might respond to such an assertion by pointing out that the speaker must at that very moment be "imposing" "relativism" on the listener. More importantly, according to Fish's view, no one's most basic values ever belong exclusively to an individual (our primary interpretive assumptions always belong to an interpretive *community*). Although such "relativism" is obviously contradictory and not really "relativism" as Fish defines it, many people continue to hold such views. More importantly, reader-response theory is incapable of considering the social effects of these contradictory beliefs. If we examine relativism, not as simply an untenable position, but as a system/anti-system of social constraints, we can begin to see how it effectively obligates an individual to hold the beliefs of all others (even those views momentarily held in common) as nothing more than "opinions." Regardless of Fish's insistence that such a position can only be held theoretically and is impossible to apply successfully, the social effect of such beliefs is to make the idea of mutual obligation incoherent. In such a society, the only obligation is to avoid appealing to any other sense of obligation. Fish's insistence that such a condition of obligation would still constitute a "constraint" does not negate the erratic influence that the failed attempts to fulfil such an impossible obligation can exert on a community.

CHAPTER THREE

[1] Because my citations are taken primarily from John Carey's translation of *De Doctrina Christiana*, I use his translation of the title, *Christian Doctrine*, rather than Fish's *The Christian Doctrine*. It should also be noted that because the present argument is concerned with how Fish reads the theological treatise as part of Milton's corpus, the recent debate over Miltonic authorship of *De Doctrina* is not relevant here. For this reason, I shall throughout my discussion here and in other chapters follow Fish's example by referring to opinions presented in the theological treatise as Milton's. My decision to write as if Milton had authored the treatise should not therefore be taken as an indication of my position with respect to that debate. For the most sustained and detailed arguments against Miltonic authorship of the treatise see William Hunter's *Visitation Unimplor'd*. See also the report by Campbell et al. for the results of an attempt to resolve the question by means of stylistic analysis. For arguments favouring the attribution see, among many others, Christopher Hill's essay, "Professor William B. Hunter, Bishop Burgess and John Milton," *SEL* 34 (1994): 165-93, and Barbara K. Lewalski's "Milton and *De Doctrina Christiana*: Evidences of Authorship," *Milton Studies* 36 (1998): 203-28. For my own assessment of this debate, specifically as it bears upon Milton's Christology and materialism, see "The *Teloi* of Genres: *Paradise Lost* and *De Doctrina Christiana*," *Milton Studies* 39 (2000), forthcoming.

[2] In a more recent essay, Campbell proposes an account similar to the one I have suggested: "it could be argued that Milton's decision to publish the *Artis Logicae* in

144

1672 was prompted by a belief that it contained the logic that would support his heterodox theology" ("Authorship" 130). Whether one agrees exactly with such an historical claim, the central issue for present purposes is that the relevant theological points with which we are concerned here have direct antecedents in the Ramist logic text. There is also a sense in which my point regarding Milton's *Artis Logicae* is then in obvious agreement with Campbell's earlier argument—that Milton's theological position is simply a function of his logical first-principles. The only difficulty in the phrasing of Campbell's earlier account is in appearing to suggest that Milton "just happened" to draw these deductions from his logic text, rather than from direct consideration of the theological issues.

[3] It should be noted here that *Paradise Lost* presents an account of rationality decidedly different from the reductive rationalism that we find ambient in the theological treatise. In my essay, "The *Teloi* of Genres," I take up the question of comparison between the epic and the treatise in some detail, contending that Milton understood and attempted to exploit the implicit and explicit disparity between the accounts of reason presumed by each of the two works. Thus, although my argument here is not determined by the debate over Miltonic authorship of *De Doctrina* (granting Fish what he presumes in this respect), those Miltonists who find my account of the theological treatise troubling may need to reconsider (or at least complicate) their view of the relation between the treatise and the rest of the Miltonic corpus.

My point here regarding the relation between Ramism and *De Doctrina* is also supported (in spite of apparent claims to the contrary) by the arguments of P. Albert Duhamel regarding "Milton's Alleged Ramism." Duhamel argues that Milton departed from Ramist orthodoxy in important ways because (following Aristotle) he viewed logic as something more "artificial" than did Ramus (1039). This point, however, strengthens my observation that Milton (whatever his relation to Ramism *per se*) was furthering the movement towards a view of knowledge (and *doctrina*) as making (*techne*). On the other hand, Duhamel's assertion, that *De Doctrina* is only "incidentally argumentative" and that Ramist method was used only as an effective means of organizing the primarily scriptural text (1047), ignores the obviously influential power of logical and taxonomic arrangement in compelling agreement. Moreover, as Brian Weiss points out, the foundation of Duhamel's argument, which basically involves tracking every instance of the use of syllogisms in all of Milton's major prose, is flawed because it is based on a mistaken understanding of the Ramist term "argument" (as though Milton's use of syllogisms demonstrates that he is not a true Ramist) (Weiss 59-62). In brief, within Ramism "argument" is a technical term more closely approximating what we would today understand as "predication": an "argument" in that sense is simply the most basic unit of discourse and "has nothing to do with polemic" *per se* (Weiss 7). Of course, a Ramist "would tend not to speak of 'predication' as this word is associated with Aristotelian predicaments" (7n). Thus, although Duhamel's central thesis about the precise character of Milton's deployment of Ramist argument is incorrect, his argument still supports my broader point regarding the way in which Milton's *De Doctrina Christiana* shares in the overall movement toward the development of instrumental rationality.

[4] Fish's argument that "self-consciousness" will always lead to false humility also concurs in part with Augustine's position. Augustine was no less sensitive than Fish to

the problems of self-reflexive infinite regress. Fish, however, falsely deduces that because we can never be "consciously" humble, humility is altogether impossible. The more precise term for use in this discussion is "meekness," referring to accurate self-knowledge (which Fish says is impossible), as distinct from "humility" which can be more directly associated with indiscriminate self-abasement. In keeping with the Augustinian view of self-knowledge, Walter Hilton (d. 1396) makes the important distinction between "imperfect meekness" (comparable to Fish's "false humility"), and "perfect meekness." The former of these, while good to some degree, suffers from the very problems that Fish mentions, in that it depends upon "intellectual self-appraisal" (Hilton 146). "Perfect" (or complete) meekness is possible, however, because we can, without self-consciousness, set our affections solely on Christ (88; 146-47). The difficulty in trying to understand Hilton's point from within Fish's terms of reference is that Fish can always reduce "affection for Christ" to rationally calculating self-interest. Fish's argument is incapable of accounting for (allowing) what is absolutely central to Augustine's thought: the desire of creature for creator. Although this Augustinian ordering of the affections does lead to meekness (accurate self-knowledge) as a matter of course, such self-knowledge is never a result of self-awareness or self-consciousness, because meekness itself is neither the goal of thought nor the object of the affections. Satan's question, "Who can think submission?" depends upon a mode of apprehension which excludes the affections, focusing solely on the rational consciousness. The question assumes that the desire of creature for creator can never be anything more than a mercenary affair. The catch is that while such a position appears to be a statement about human (or angelic) nature (seeing egoism as inescapable) it actually depends more basically upon a specific view of God: the belief that there is no grace.

5   The most obvious element that Fish *does* borrow from Mazzeo is his emphasis upon Neoplatonic motifs in Augustine's writing (Mazzeo 1, 23-27). The problem with Mazzeo's reading is that it effectively ignores the centrality of the incarnation in Augustine's thought, by making him into a Platonist (22-26) (see Copleston 73-74, as well as my argument on 68-70 for an alternative view). Donald Marshall also points out that Mazzeo's Neoplatonic reading of Augustine (privileging the contemplative life) is contradicted by much of Augustine's active life as a preacher (Marshall 2). Marshall points out that Augustine does not subscribe to the "philosophic" (Platonic) view of language as a first (inadequate) step up towards the "higher ontological plane" (12). Instead, because Augustine's understanding of language is informed by *caritas*, he emphasizes the relational and conventional constitution of language (12-13). However, although "signs are not valid among men except by consent," that consent can be for good or evil purposes (13). In this way, Augustine avoids allowing a conventional view of language to remove the ability to distinguish between good and evil (13; cf. Louth 157-58). The tendency to read Augustine as simply a Platonist (or a proto-Saussurian) results from a failure to recognize that the role of *caritas* for Augustine is not primarily logical. Hence, although James Murphy notes the importance of *caritas* for Augustine's theory, he still emphasizes the importance of the "individual learner" (*Rhetoric in the Middle Ages* 287) or "individual judgement" ("Metarhetorics" 207), to such an extent that he thinks Augustine "encourages private interpretation of messages" (207). Murphy rightly emphasizes the full relational dimensions of *caritas* in Augustine's re-orientation of rhetoric (*RMA* 289-91), but he does not connect the importance

146

of *caritas* to Augustine's more basic understanding of the sign. Augustine insists that the communication of *caritas* requires human relations (*DDC* Prol. 6), but Murphy's treatment of the *De Doctrina* does not apply that qualification to the doctrine of signs (Murphy, "Metarhetorics" 207; *RMA* 286-87). Similarly, Murphy's treatment of *De Magistro* overlooks the fact that the very form of the work (as a dialogue) contradicts an individualist reading (*RMA* 287).

6   My point here is similar to that made by Brenda Deen Schildgen in "Augustine's Response to Jacques Derrida." Schildgen argues that the "fundamentally [anti]theological position" of Derrida depends upon first equating belief in God with a belief in completely determined textual meaning (Schildgen 384-87). Refutation of the latter is then be taken as a refutation of the former. The poststructuralist misreading overlooks Augustine's emphasis upon the very "mediate" (interpretive and debatable, rather than "immediate") nature of all human communication (388-93). The key step in Derrida's argument (as with so many others) is in his application of "Platonic schema" to Augustine's position (389).

7   At root here is the difference between Fish and Augustine on the issue of the human "will," a matter to be discussed more fully in chapter 7. Already we can note that, in keeping with the general tendency of most postmodern thinkers, Fish does not dismiss consideration of the will, but simply assumes its irrelevance. The difficulty here is that the concept of "will" commonly ignored/dismissd is assumed to be the free will of the autonomous liberal subject and has no relation to the sophisticated Augustinian analysis of human motivation amidst manifold constraints. Rather, Augustine's notion of the will is intimately connected to his thinking about *caritas*, but that too is a term the content of which Fish deems interminably debatable. This is why the issue cannot be addressed until after we have more fully considered the claims of Augustinian *caritas* in chapter 5. Moreover, any discussion of the relation between the two respective positions will need to go in a direction altogether different from the platitudes usually recited in the "free will vs. determinism" debate, because Fish rejects both the theological implications of a free will yet also claims to reject the rationalism upon which determinism usually depends. In *The Life of the Mind*, Hannah Arendt offers one of the better analyses of Augustine's view of the will, in which she engages all of Augustine's main treatments of the topic in view of his *Retractationes* (Arendt 84-110).

CHAPTER FOUR

1   Earlier I pointed out that this later alignment of "philosophy" (rather than rhetoric) with formal logic (objectivism) is a reversal of the position that Fish initially offered in *Self-Consuming Artifacts*, where he aligns formal logic with the rhetoricians. While this reversal within Fish's argument turns upon a realignment of the "complacent status quo" from the rhetorician's position to the objectivist's position, there is a further sense in which Fish is also benefiting from an unresolved tension within the Platonic corpus, between the *Phaedrus* and the *Republic*, regarding the relation between textuality (objectification) and reason (*logos* as *ratio* and *oratio*) (Ong, *Orality* 167-68).

2   There is no opportunity to delineate here the differing accounts of the continuity or discontinuity between ancient and modern rationalism. It is sufficient to

observe that the present argument differs from both the Nietzschean account which subsumes Christianity within a continuous rationalist tradition from Plato to the moderns (Nietzsche 64, 125, 236-42, 308), and from the Straussian account which emphasizes the break between ancient and modern rationalism. According to Strauss, the central difference between ancient and modern rationalism lies in the classical emphasis upon understanding the limitations of human beings within nature, as opposed to the modern attempt to overcome nature (chance) altogether (Strauss 85-86). Because of the modern belief in the human ability to master nature by means of reason, "reason replaces nature" as the basis for understanding good (88, 92). Because Strauss's account is concerned with the difference between ancient and modern thinking, he does not always emphasize the deeper continuity between them which is relevant to the present argument: they are both primarily concerned with an understanding of *nature* as the object and matrix of human knowing. Elsewhere Strauss does discuss the central difference between what he calls "reason and revelation" (298-310). But even in that context Strauss does not emphasize this deeper continuity between ancient and modern philosophy.

3 In *What's Wrong with Postmodernism*, Christopher Norris makes a point similar to my argument regarding Fish's inadvertent dependence upon the Ramist bifurcation of rhetoric and logic. Norris observes (taking a cue from Paul de Man) that Fish "equates rhetoric with language in its purely suasive dimension" (110), and thereby ignores the "cognitive" aspect of "rhetoric as a form of immanent critique" (109; cf. Norris, *Spinoza* 152). This may seem to resemble my point that Fish follows Ramus, not only in the arbitrary division between rhetoric and logic, but in the suppression of the importance of reason as a consitutive element within rhetoric. But the difference between my criticism and that of Norris (via de Man) is that by accessing this aspect of Fish's argument through Ramist/Miltonic analogues I can avoid some of the textualist reductions still implicit in the work of Norris and de Man (Norris, *Spinoza* 152).

4 To those who are familiar with Derrida's broader account of "ontotheology," my use of his phrasing here (in connection with the doctrine of the Trinity) might seem misleading if not openly perverse. Particularly in *Dissemination*, Derrida states explicitly that his own triadic response to the aporias of the presence-absence binary must be sharply distinguished from the "three of ontotheology" (25; cf. 352-53). The root of the problem according to Derrida is that the Trinity of Christian theology is still part of the metaphysical (Platonic) tradition that insists upon complete presence. We cannot address Derrida's position in detail here, but two points are worth noting. First, insofar as Derrida's position follows the general contours of the poststructuralist account of the Christian position (i.e., shaped by the Heideggerian metanarrative of Western culture derived from what is unsaid in Nietzsche), his argument proceeds from a basic misapprehension of the Trinity and Christianity in general—construed as Platonism for the masses. Second, Derrida's assumed account of the Trinity does not allow for the brokenness of the Second Person—the God who suffers with and in creation and experiences its lack and abandonment.

148

[1] I should point out that I am not using Descartes here (or in the earlier citations) as simply a scapegoat to represent the "bad foundationalist." Indeed, there is much in Descartes' work that preserves and continues what might be called the "Platonic-Augustinian theological tradition." However, although influences and inter-relationships abound between the texts of Descartes, Augustine and Plato, our concern here is to observe the more important differences which are too often over-looked.

[2] In attempting to distinguish sufficiently between Augustine's position and that of modern objectivism, there is some danger that Augustine may start to appear as a subjectivist (or that I may be thought to misrepresent him as such). I must therefore emphasize that I am not suggesting that Augustine subscribed to anything that a modern would recognize as subjectivism. What I have been trying to show is that radical subjectivism (solipsism etc.) is really only an inverse function of the same reductive rationalism in which Augustine never participates. In further response to Fish's position on this point, Bill Readings' analysis corroborates my argument regarding the risk of solipsism. Readings points out that Fish's appeal specifically to sophist rhetoric as a model for pedagogy "risks turning the pedagogic relation back into a site of subjective calculation" which seeks to "erase the pole of the addressee" (by making it identical with that of the speaker) (159). Readings goes on to develop his own basis for pedagogical practice by describing the "referent of teaching" as "the name of Thought." By replacing "the empty idea of excellence [in the techno-bureaucratic sense] with the empty name of Thought," Readings argues that "a *self-conscious* exposure of the emptiness of Thought" (i.e., its lack of inherent meaning) can replace "vulgarity with honesty" (159-60; emphasis added). The primary difficulty here is that Readings depends upon the same privileging of critical self-awareness that Fish critiques so thoroughly in *Doing What Comes Naturally*. In effect, the ability of people to be "honest" about the true emptiness of the name of Thought, presumes that we can "catch ourselves introspecting," as it were, long enough for even the honesty of vacuity to function. That is, it still depends upon claiming that our very awareness of contextual embeddedness enables some kind of freedom from those interpretive/historical constraints which constitute that perception.

[3] As indicated earlier, the recent debate initiated by William Hunter over the extent of Miltonic authorship of *De Doctrina Christiana* is not relevant to the present argument because we are concerned ultimately with Fish's use of Milton (see 144 n1, above). I should also point out here that the argument being advanced thus far is restricted to Milton's prose works and specifically to the logical and theological texts under consideration. The present analysis does not directly consider *Paradise Lost* (for example) because, instead of treating Milton's *De Doctrina* as a gloss on his poetry, I have tried to approach the work within its self-proclaimed terms of reference as a piece of Reformation theology. The attempt to substantiate claims regarding Milton's deployment of the principle of reason in his works more broadly would require a qualitatively different kind of argument than the one being offered here. Thus when I characterize Milton's position on a given point, it should be understood with reference to the assumptions and implications of the doctrinal treatise (to which Fish appeals) and granted that my account would need to be modified in important ways if it were to consider Milton's corpus as a whole (see 145 n3).

[4] In chapter 3 I noted the way in which the chirographic control of Learned Latin tended to encourage the understanding of words as "objects seen" rather than "speech heard." We can begin to get some sense of the theological implications of this linguistic development by noting the differences between Milton's and Augustine's use of the same title, *De Doctrina Christiana*. In the notes to the Yale translation of Milton's treatise, Maurice Kelly offers the following observation on the differences between the two titles:

> Augustine's *De Doctrina* is a manual of Christian rhetoric designed to give the preacher both the substance and form for sermons. Milton's treatise, as his prefatory epistle shows, is his attempt to ascertain what is safely to be believed in the Christian religion. As he employs the term *doctrina*, it is synonymous with "dogma." (*CD* 125)

This shift in usage of the term *doctrina* is straightforward; however, it represents a deeper shift in thinking about language which bears directly upon broader epistemic and theological issues. Milton explicitly states that his intention is to restructure the scriptural text as a "complete corpus of doctrine, conceived in terms of a definite course of instruction" (128):

> I aim only to assist the reader's memory by collecting together, as it were, into a single book texts which are scattered here and there throughout the Bible, and by systematizing them under definite headings, in order to make reference easy. (127)

Again Ramist logical method looms large in Milton's theology, while the mention of "collecting" reminds us of the active interpretive project that Fish notes in the *Doctrine and Discipline of Divorce* ("Wanting" 54). William Schullenberger links the above passage from the *De Doctrina* with Milton's appropriation of the Myth of Osiris in *Areopagitica*:

> From that time [after the apostles] ever since, the sad friends of Truth, such as durst appear, imitating the careful search that Isis made for the mangled body of Osiris, went up and down gathering up limb by limb still as they could find them. We have not yet found them all, Lords and Commons, nor ever shall do, till her Master's second coming. (*Areopagitica* 742)

Schullenberger observes that the goal of Milton's theological project "is to construct an approximation of that lost original doctrine" (277). However, Schullenberger never points out that the success of Milton's analogy makes "doctrine" a dead body. *De Doctrina Christiana* for Milton is the attempt to reassemble a dismembered corpse, whereas *De Doctrina Christiana* for Augustine is ultimately the verbal expression of *caritas*. This is not to accuse Milton of "poor usage," but simply to point out the consequences of doing theology in a language which had had no native speakers for over a thousand years (Ong, *Orality* 163-64). The shift from a primarily active to a primarily substantive understanding of *doctrina* is not as important for what it tells us about Milton specifically, as for what it indicates regarding the theological tradition (historical interpretive community) in which Milton's *De Doctrina* participates. (For further analysis of the lexical range in Augustine's use of the term *doctrina*, see G. A. Press, "Doctrina.")

This same calcification of language resulting from chirographic control of Latin is also reflected in the Renaissance debates over the translation of the New Testament *logos*. Contrary to Sloane's claim that "for Augustine [*logos*] is always ver-

bum never *sermo*" (108), Erasmus observes that Augustine uses both *verbum* and *sermo* for *logos* (Boyle 16). The relevant point here is that by the Renaissance period, the Learned Latin usage of *verbum* was no longer capable of bearing the same sense of orality implied in using the Greek *logos* to translate the Hebrew *dabar* (Boyle 24; Ong, *Rhetoric* 2). Whether or not Erasmus was prudent in changing *verbum* to *sermo* (a usage Milton follows) in his translation of John 1:1, the point remains that between Augustine and Erasmus, usage of the term *verbum* shifted so as to make it incapable of indicating the spoken (and living) quality which it implied in Augustine's time.

5 Hereafter the term *caritas*, rather than "charity," will be used to indicate Augustine's position, because of the tendency in modern English usage for "charity" to be associated exclusively with actions rather than affections. It is important to emphasize that Augustine's notion of *caritas* still includes much of the action we would generally associate with the term "charity." However, precisely because Augustine never separates affection from the ultimate *telos* of our actions, I shall use the term *caritas*. I shall also use the term *caritas* rather than *agape*, because we are concerned primarily with Augustine's "Latin understanding" of *agape* as *caritas*, and because the question of Augustine's knowledge of Greek will probably remain unanswerable (Johnson 218-19).

6 Thomas Sloane places Fish "among the many interpreters who believe that Augustine does not discuss rhetoric until the fourth book" of *De Doctrina* (301), although Fish's attempt to link Augustine's discussion of "use vs. enjoyment" (in book 1) with the opposition of "dialectic vs. rhetoric" shows that Sloane is not entirely correct. Sloane's own argument is that "Augustine shatters the integrity of rhetoric not by counterposing it with dialectic but by blinding it with the Light, with an unmistakeable, *a priori* truth" (301; 107). Sloane is right to emphasize the primacy of *caritas* in Augustine's thinking (107), but he seems to miss his own point (here at least) by immediately making the ability for *caritas* to provide a (quasi-rationalist) logical premise its principal function.

7 Although I have benefitted much from William Hunter's discussion of these issues, my reading of this particular passage from Milton's *De Doctrina* differs from his. Hunter maintains that in the above block quotation (from *CD* 140-42), Milton is consistent with the point that he makes in *Artis Logicae* regarding the distinction between "essence proper" (or "form") and the particular existent that comes into being when *prima materia* (as *substantia ex Deo*) is embued with form (*AL* 232-34). I agree completely with Hunter's account of this distinction in relation to creatures. However, in this particular passage of *De Doctrina* where he is discussing God's essence, Milton can and does (in a qualitifed way) equate essence with substance (and hypostasis) specifically because God is uncreated and thus does not come into existence by being differentiated out of his own substance (cf. Hunter, "Definitions" 16). For a further account of Milton's deployment of the term "substance" in relation to creaturely existence, see my paper, "'Matter' versus Body: The Character of Milton's Monism," *Milton Quarterly* 33.3 (1999): 79-85.

8 Milton does also treat Colossians 1:15-17, but he does so in a manner similar to his handling of John 1:1-3. By insisting that there is no logical difference between being "begotten" and being "made," Milton maintains that the desig-

151

nation "firstborn of creation" means only that Christ is created first (asserting that both must occur within time) (*CD* 261-62).

9   I should also clarify here that although my argument draws upon Ong's work on Ramus (in relation to typographic developments) and on the chirographic character of Learned Latin, it does not necessarily depend at all upon his thesis regarding the existence (hypothetical or not) of "primary oral cultures."

CHAPTER SEVEN

1   Some readers may indeed be wondering why this study has not dealt sooner and in more detail with what is arguably still Fish's most widely influential book. There were two basic reasons for not engaging more directly the arguments of *Surprised by Sin*: first, as noted in the Introduction, the nature of the initial theoretical question posed by Fish's arguments dictated that the very constitution of a text like *Paradise Lost* was at issue; second, the nature of those arguments required that we focus on his more explicitly theoretical analyses that only really developed after *Surprised by Sin*. In *Surprised by Sin* Fish does make the same historical point that he makes in *Self-Consuming Artifacts*, explicitly linking Augustine's *De Doctrina* with the Platonic understanding of dialectical transformation (*SS* 342-43). But only in his later work do we find a complete argument against the mind-independent reality of the text, an argument made possible only by reversing his previous characterization of the rhetoric-philosophy opposition, effectively subsuming the latter within Enlightenment rationalism. Of course, for Miltonists, the fact remains that *Surprised by Sin* has been the single most influential work in Milton studies over the last quarter-century. As John Rumrich points out, the continued breadth and depth of Fish's influence is evidenced by the way in which many of the most apparently opposed current readings of Milton still take as their starting point a view of the poet and his work largely shaped by the arguments of *Surprised by Sin* (Rumrich 2-10)—a view that Rumrich explicitly undertakes to refute in *Milton Unbound.*

2   What is so deeply misleading about even such an off-hand comment like Fish's is the fact that, for someone like Augustine who actually did come to believe in the doctrine of original sin, such a belief did not in any way dictate a belief in "determinate" textual meaning. As we established in chapter 3, Augustine no less insisted upon the humanly rooted nature of linguistic signs, even as he insited upon the mind-independent reality of the ends that they served.

3   I make this point *not* to suggest that Fish is ignorant of the Augustinian category of memory or its important differences from the Platonic tradition. Indeed, in *Self-Consuming Artifacts* Fish notes precisely those differences and discusses how John Donne plays these two conceptions of memory off one another (*SCA* 45-51). The relevant point here is that in formulating his theoretical arguments later on, Fish could have avoided collapsing knowledge into awareness if he had consulted his own book of memory.

4   It should be added here that the present drive in many North American University departments of English toward the instituting of courses exclusively focused on "essay writing" is in perfect accord with the technological imperative for contentless form— i.e., training in the rhetorical technique that will predictably get the desired results.

5   A third aspect of that dynamic tension (not emphasized here but which is customarily part of any theological treatment of such issues) is the operation of the Holy Spirit, who together with the truth of the message enables the believing community to incarnate *caritas* in the present. It should also be noted that there is no necessary opposition between the operation of the elements that make up the personal process described above (whether events, capacities, persons or narratives) and the work of grace, for those very elements *are* some of the means of grace, and as such can be accepted or refused.

6   In this aspect of Fish's argument there is a striking similarity between his position and the attempts by various seventeenth-century English clerics to separate altogether the claims of morality from the content of specific theological claims. Although such attempts usually began in an adiaphorist spirit of trying to establish exactly what constituted "things indifferent" in matters of religion, they often became attempts to establish certain moral principles as completely independent from all religious claims. The irony of such a project is evident in the influence of the Cambridge Platonists (e.g., Benjamin Whichcote), who despite their explicit attempts to the contrary, ended up becoming absorbed in the broader sweep of deism. The extremity of the Cambridge Platonists' emphasis upon virtuous action as the core of religion led them to reject all forms of dogmatism on principle. The problem with such a position is that it presupposes a radical distinction between will and understanding which eventually leads to a kind of voluntarism that abjures all that is normally considered the content of "faith." Such a view incorporates into its foundations the very thing it attempts to reject because it depends upon a notion that "faith" consists primarily of dogma (propositions) that can then be separated from ethical "action." The Cambridge Platonists explicitly rejected precisely such a view of faith, but in doing so they simply isolated the realm of ethical action and thereby reinforced the view that the content of the dogma really does have no relation to ethical considerations in the first place. My argument has been that, although a person's ethical action may be divorced from one's ostensible belief, the disjunction is not a necessary one because ethical actions do depend upon what a person genuinely believes. For example, there are numerous concrete and far-reaching ethical implications for a Christian who believes in the credal "resurrection of the dead"—both Christ's and the believer's—but the degree of one's accordance with those implications will depend in part upon the extent of one's faith (as well as understanding).

7   I use the term "secular" in its precise Augustinian sense, based on a reading of *City of God* influenced initially by R. A. Markus's detailed study entitled *Saeculum: History and Society in the Theology of St. Augustine* (see esp. 101-51) and more recently by Oliver O'Donovan's response to Markus in essay form and in *The Desire of the Nations*. The basic point here is that the Augustinian sense of the term "secular" should not be confused with the modern liberal sense in which the term is used: (1) to refer to institutions (O'Donovan, "Augustine's" 141); and (2) to contrast with the "sacred" (*Desire* 211). Moreover, the *saeculum* that Augustine describes is not to be identified with the "City of Man" (which is set in opposition to the "City of God") (Markus 101-02). Rather, *saeculum* is simply the temporally limited "earthly peace," "a condition of order that is common to both communities" (O'Donovan, "Augustine's" 141). In this respect, the *saeculum* embraces all humans within time—this is why Augustine insists upon the "eschatological

153

ambivalence of all empirical human groupings" (Markus 151; *City of God* 20.7). The key point for present purposes is that the Augustinian account of *saeculum* insists upon human temporal limitation. Most importantly, although theological reflection is, of course, no less limited than literary reflection by the constraints of human capacities (always flawed, always partial), the correct ordering of the affections requires that neither kind of reflection should be confused with or substituted for the charitable end which either discourse may potentially serve (or not). Here again we find the daring subtlety with which Fish has consistently appropriated the Miltonic-Augustinian imperative to avoid ascribing eternal status to merely temporal things, by drawing a parallel between such a theological position and his own account of the self-contained character of professional practice. The parallel is striking, but again with one crucial difference: the "secular" (in the Augustinian sense), or temporally limited, character of human discourses is rooted for Augustine in the apprehension that such discourses are not ultimate specifically because something else—human participation in the *caritas* of God—is. Moreover, because of the Incarnation there is the possibility of interaction between human finitude and *caritas*. Fish's professionalism, by contrast, is predicated on the assertion that because nothing could be ultimate, the only human possibility is to move between various self-contained discursive spheres—each of them disallowing the relevance of the claim to serve anything beyond themselves.

WORKS CITED

Aers, David. and Bob Hodge. "'Rational Burning': Milton on Sex and Marriage." *Milton Studies* 13 (1979): 3-33.

Arendt, Hannah. *The Life of the Mind.* New York: Harcourt Brace Jovanovich, 1978.

Aristotle. *Nicomachean Ethics.* Trans. Terence Irwin. Indianapolis: Hackett, 1985.

Augustine, St. *Confessions.* Trans. R. S. Pine-Coffin. Markham: Penguin, 1961.

——. *De Doctrina Christiana Libri IV.* Ed. Josephus Martin. *Corpus Christianorum, Series Latina.* Vol. 32. Turnholti: Typographi Brepols Editores Pontificii, 1962.

——. *On Christian Doctrine.* Trans. D. W. Robertson. New York: Macmillan, 1958.

——. *On the Trinity.* Trans. Arthur West Haddan. *A Select Library of the Nicene and Post-Nicene Fathers of the Christian Church, Vol. 3.* Ed. Philip Schaff. Grand Rapids, MI: Eerdmans, 1993. 1-228.

——. *Homilies on the Gospel of John.* Trans. John Gibb and James Innes. *A Select Library of the Nicene and Post-Nicene Fathers of the Christian Church, Vol. 7.* Ed. Philip Schaff. Grand Rapids, MI: Eerdmans, 1983. 1-456.

Barash, Carol Isaacson. "The Use and Abuse of Legal Theory: A Reply to Fish." *Philosophy and Social Criticism* 15.2 (1989): 183-97.

Bauman, Michael. *A Scripture Index to John Milton's "De Doctrina Christiana."* Binghampton, NY: Medieval and Renaissance Texts and Sudies, 1989.

Boyle, Marjorie O'Rourke. *Erasmus on Language and Method in Theology.* Toronto: U of Toronto P, 1977.

Campbell, Gordon. "The Authorship of *De Doctrina Christiana.*" *Milton Quarterly* 26.4 (1992): 129-30.

——. "The Son of God in *De Doctrina Christiana* and *Paradise Lost.*" *Modern Language Review* 75.3 (1980): 507-14.

Campbell, Gordon, et al. *Milton and "De Doctrina Christiana."* On-line. U of Ohio. Internet. 5 Oct. 1996. Available: http://voyager.cns.ohiou.edu./~somalley/ddc.html

Carney, James D. "Literary Relativism." *Journal of Aesthetic Education* 21.3 (1987): 5-16.

Cochrane, Charles Norris. *Christianity and Classical Culture: A Study of Thought and Action from Augustus to Augustine.* New York: Oxford UP, 1957.

Copenhaver, Brian P. and Charles B. Schmitt. *Renaissance Philosophy. A History of Western Philosophy, Vol. 3.* Oxford: Oxford UP, 1992.

Copleston, Frederick. *A History of Philosophy, Vol. 2: Mediaeval Philosophy Part 1: Augustine to Bonaventure.* Garden City, NY: Image Books, 1962.

Currie, Gregory. "Text Without Context: Some Errors of Stanley Fish." *Philosophy and Literature* 15 (1991): 212-28.

Derrida, Jacques. *Dissemination.* Trans. Barbara Johnson. Chicago: U of Chicago P, 1981.

—— *Writing and Difference.* Trans. Alan Bass. Chicago: U of Chicago P, 1978.

Descartes, René. *Meditationes de Prima Philosophia / Meditations of First Philosophy: A Bilingual Edition.* Ed. and Trans. George Heffernan. Notre Dame: U of Notre Dame P, 1990.

155

Donnelly, Phillip J. "'Matter' versus Body: The Character of Milton's Monism." *Milton Quarterly* 33.3 (1999): 79-85.

—. "The *Teloi* of Genres: *Paradise Lost* and *De Doctrina Christiana*." *Milton Studies* 39 (2000), forthcoming.

Doull, James A. "Augustinian Trinitarianism and Existential Theology." *Dionysius* 3 (1979): 111-59.

Duhamel, P. Albert. "Milton's Alleged Ramism." *PMLA* 67 (1952): 1035-53.

Eagleton, Terry. "The Ideology of the Aesthetic." *The Politics of Pleasure: Aesthetics and Cultural Theory.* Ed. Stephan Regan. Buckingham, PA: Open UP, 1992. 17-31.

Erickson, Millard J. *Christian Theology.* Grand Rapids, MI: Baker Book House, 1985.

Fish, Stanley. *Doing What Comes Naturally: Change, Rhetoric, and the Practice of Theory in Literary and Legal Studies.* Oxford: Oxford UP, 1989.

—. "Driving from the Letter: Truth and Indeterminacy in Milton's Areopagitica." *Re-membering Milton: Essays on the Texts and Traditions.* Ed. Mary Nyquist and Margaret W. Ferguson. London: Methuen, 1988. 234-54.

—. *Is There a Text in This Class? The Authority of Interpretive Communities.* Cambridge, MA: Harvard UP, 1980.

—. *Professional Correctness: Literary Studies and Political Change.* New York: Oxford UP, 1995.

—. *Self-Consuming Artifacts: The Experience of Seventeenth-Century Literature.* Berkeley: U of California P, 1972.

—. *Surprised by Sin: The Reader in "Paradise Lost."* 2nd ed. London: MacMillan, 1997.

—. *There's No Such Thing as Free Speech: And It's a Good Thing Too.* Oxford: Oxford UP, 1994.

—. "Wanting a Supplement: The Question of Interpretation in Milton's Early Prose." *Politics, Poetics and Hermeneutics in Milton's Prose.* Ed. David Loewenstein and James Grantham Turner. New York: Cambridge UP, 1990. 41-68.

Gilson, Etienne. *The Christian Philosophy of Saint Augustine.* Trans. L. E. M. Lynch. New York: Vintage Books, 1960.

Grant, George. *Technology and Justice.* Concord, ON: Anansi, 1986.

Gunton, Colin. "Augustine, the Trinity and the Theological Crisis of the West." *Scottish Journal of Theology* 43 (1990): 33-58.

Harris, Roy and Talbot J. Taylor. *Landmarks in Linguistic Thought.* New York: Routledge, 1989.

Hill, Christopher. "Professor William B. Hunter, Bishop Burgess and John Milton." *SEL* 34 (1994): 165-93.

Hilton, Walter. *Toward a Perfect Love: The Spiritual Counsel of Walter Hilton.* Trans. David L. Jeffrey. Portland, OR: Multnoma, 1985.

Hunter, William B. "Further Definitions: Milton's Theological Vocabulary." *Bright Essence: Studies in Milton's Theology.* Ed. William B. Hunter, C. A. Patrides and J. H. Adamson. Salt Lake City: U of Utah P, 1971. 15-25.

—. *Visitation Unimplor'd: Milton and the Authorship of "De Doctrina Christiana."* Pittsburgh: Duquesne UP, 1998.

Inglis, Fred. *Cultural Studies.* Oxford: Oxford UP, 1993.

156

Iser, Wolfgang. *The Implied Reader.* Baltimore: Johns Hopkins UP, 1974.

Jauss, Hans Robert. *Toward an Aesthetic of Reception.* Trans. Timothy Bahti. Minneapolis: U of Minnesota P, 1982.

Johnson, W. R. "Isocrates Flowering: The Rhetoric of Augustine." *Philosophy and Rhetoric* 9.4 (1976): 217-31.

Kenshur, Oscar. "The Rhetoric of Incommensurability." *Journal of Aesthetics and Art Criticism* 42.4 (1984): 375-81.

Kroeker, P. Travis. *Christian Ethics and Political Economy in North America: A Critical Analysis.* Montreal: McGill-Queens UP, 1995.

Lewalski, Barbara K. "Milton and *De Doctrina Christiana*: Evidences of Authorship." *Milton Studies* 36 (1998): 203-28.

Louth, Andrew. "Augustine on Language." *Journal of Literature and Theology* 3.2 (1989): 151-58.

MacIntyre, Alasdair. *Three Rival Versions of Moral Inquiry.* Notre Dame: U of Notre Dame P, 1990.

Markus, R. A. *Saeculum: History and Society in the Theology of St. Augustine.* Cambridge: Cambridge UP, 1970.

Marshall, Donald G. "Making Letters Speak: Interpreter as Orator in Augustine's *De Doctrina Christiana.*" *Religion and Literature* 24.2 (1992): 1-17.

Mazzeo, Joseph A. "St. Augustine's Rhetoric of Silence: Truth vs. Eloquence and Things vs. Signs." *Renaissance and Seventeenth Century Studies.* New York: Columbia UP, 1964. 1-28.

Meynell, Hugo. "Fish Fingered: Anatomy of a Deconstructionist." *Journal of Aesthetic Education* 23.2 (1989): 5-15.

Milton, John. *Areopagitica. The Complete Prose Works of John Milton, Vol. 2.* Ed. Ernest Sirluck. New Haven: Yale UP, 1959. 480-570.

——. *Christian Doctrine.* Trans. John Carey. *Complete Prose Works of John Milton, Vol. 6.* Ed. Maurice Kelly. New Haven: Yale UP, 1973.

——. *De Doctrina Christiana.* Trans. Charles R. Sumner. *The Works of John Milton, Vol. 14.* New York: Columbia UP, 1933.

——. *Doctrine and Discipline of Divorce. The Complete Prose Works of John Milton, Vol. 2.* Ed. Ernest Sirluck. New Haven: Yale UP, 1959. 217-356.

——. *A Fuller Course in the Art of Logic.* Trans. and Eds. Walter J. Ong and Charles J. Ermatinger. *Complete Prose Works of John Milton, Vol. 8.* New Haven: Yale UP, 1982. 139-407.

——. *Of Prelatical Episcopacy. The Complete Prose Works of John Milton, Vol. 1.* Ed. Don M. Wolfe. New Haven: Yale UP, 1953. 618-52.

——. *Paradise Lost. John Milton: Complete Poems and Major Prose.* Ed. Merritt Y. Hughes. New York: Macmillan, 1957. 173-469.

Murphy, James J. "The Metarhetorics of Plato, Augustine, and McLuhan: A Pointing Essay." *Philosophy and Rhetoric* 4.4 (1971): 201-14.

——. *Rhetoric in the Middle Ages: A History of Rhetorical Theory from Saint Augustine to the Renaissance.* Berkeley: U of California P, 1974.

New English Bible: The Apocrypha. Cambridge: Oxford UP and Cambridge UP, 1970.

Nietzsche, Friedrich. *The Will to Power.* Trans. Walter Kaufmann and R. J. Hollingdale. Ed. Walter Kaufmann. New York: Vintage Books, 1967.

Norris, Christopher. *Spinoza and the Origins of Modern Critical Theory.* Oxford: Basil Blackwell, 1991.

—. *Uncritical Theory: Postmodernism, Intellectuals and the Gulf War.* Amherst: U of Massachusetts P, 1992.

—. *What's Wrong With Postmodernism: Critical Theory and the Ends of Philosophy.* Baltimore: Johns Hopkins UP, 1990.

O'Donovan, Oliver. "Augustine's *City of God* XIX and Western Political Thought." *Dionysius* 11 (1987): 89-110.

—. *The Desire of the Nations: Rediscovering the Roots of Political Theology.* Cambridge: Cambridge UP, 1996.

Ong, Walter J. Introduction. *A Fuller Course in the Art of Logic.* By John Milton. Ed. and Trans. Walter J. Ong and Charles J. Ermatinger. *Complete Prose Works of John Milton, Vol. 8.* New Haven: Yale UP, 1982. 144-216.

—. *Orality and Literacy: The Technologizing of the Word.* New York: Methuen, 1982.

—. *Ramus: Method and the Decay of Dialogue: From the Art of Discourse to the Art of Reason.* Cambridge, MA: Harvard UP, 1958.

—. *Rhetoric, Romance and Technology: Studies in the Interaction of Expression and Culture.* Ithaca: Cornell UP, 1971.

Plato. *Gorgias.* Trans. Walter Hamilton. Markham, Ont.: Penguin, 1960.

—. *Republic.* Trans. Allan Bloom. New York: Basic Books, 1991.

Poland, Lynn M. "Augustine, Allegory, and Conversion." *Journal of Literature and Theology* 2.1 (1988): 37-48.

Press, Gerald A. "Doctrina in Augustine's *De Doctrina Christiana.*" *Philosophy and Rhetoric* 17.2 (1984): 98-119.

Readings, Bill. *The University in Ruins.* Cambridge, MA: Harvard UP, 1996.

Ricoeur, Paul. "The Image of God and Epic of Man." *History and Truth.* Trans. Charles A. Kelby. Evanston: Northwestern UP, 1965. 110-28.

Robertson, Jr., D. W. Translator's Introduction. *On Christian Doctrine.* By Saint Augustine. New York: Macmillan, 1958. ix-xxi.

Rumrich, John P. *Milton Unbound: Controversy and Reinterpretation.* Cambridge: Cambridge UP, 1996.

Schildgen, Brenda Deen. "Augustine's Answer to Jacques Derrida in the *De Doctrina Christiana.*" *New Literary History* 25 (1994): 383-97.

Schullenberger, William. "Linguistic and Poetic Theory in Milton's *De Doctrina Christiana.*" *English Language Notes* 19.3 (1982): 262-78.

Schwartz, Regina M. "Citation, Authority, and *De Doctrina Christiana.*" *Politics, Poetics and Hermeneutics in Milton's Prose.* Ed. David Loewenstein and James Grantham Turner. New York: Cambridge UP, 1990. 227-40.

Sloane, Thomas O. *Donne, Milton, and the End of Humanist Rhetoric.* Berkeley: U of California P, 1985.

Steiner, George. *Real Presences.* Chicago: U of Chicago P, 1989.

Strauss, Leo. *An Introduction to Political Philosophy: Ten Essays by Leo Strauss.* Ed. Hilail Gildin. Detroit: Wayne State UP, 1989.

Strong, Augustus Hopkins. *Systematic Theology: A Compendium.* Westwood, NJ: Fleming H. Revell, 1907.

Vessey, Mark. "Erasmus' Jerome: The Publishing of a Christian Author." *Erasmus of Rotterdam Society Yearbook* 14 (1994): 62-99.

Weiss, Brian. "Milton's Use of Ramist Method in his Scholarly Writings." Ph.D. Diss., City Univeristy of New York, 1974.

ENGLISH LITERARY STUDIES MONOGRAPH SERIES
FOR 2000

ENGLISH LITERARY STUDIES publishes peer-reviewed monographs (usual length 45,000-60,000 words) on the literatures written in English. The Series is open to a wide range of scholarly and critical methodologies, and it considers for publication bibliographies, scholarly editions, and historical and critical studies of significant authors, texts, and issues. For a complete back-list and information for prospective contributors, see the ELS home-page: <http://www.engl.uvic.ca/els>.